Harry H. Epstein
and the Rabbinate
as Conduit for Change

Harry H. Epstein and the Rabbinate as Conduit for Change

Mark K. Bauman

Rutherford ● Madison ● Teaneck
Fairleigh Dickinson University Press
London and Toronto: Associated University Presses

Associated University Presses
440 Forsgate Drive
Cranbury, NJ 08512

Associated University Presses
25 Sicilian Avenue
London WC1A 2QH, England

Associated University Presses
P.O. Box 338, Port Credit
Mississauga, Ontario
Canada L5G 4L8

The paper used in this publication meets the requirements
of the American National Standard for Permanence of Paper
for Printed Library Materials Z39.48-1984.

Library of Congress Cataloging-in-Publication Data

Bauman, Mark K., 1946–
    Harry H. Epstein and the rabbinate as conduit for change / Mark K. Bauman.
      p. cm.
    Includes bibliographical references and index.
    ISBN 0-8386-3541-5 (alk. paper)
    1. Epstein, Harry H. (Harry Hyman), 1903– . 2. Rabbis—Georgia—Atlanta—Biography. 3. Atlanta (Ga.)—Biography. 4. Rabbis—United States—Office. 5. Conservative Judaism—United States—History. I. Title.
BM755.E687B39   1994
296.8′342′092—dc20
[B]
                                             92-55112
                                               CIP

PRINTED IN THE UNITED STATES OF AMERICA

Contents

Preface

During the winter of 1986 Mrs. Jane Leavey of the Atlanta Jewish Federation contacted me concerning the possibility of interviewing Rabbi Harry H. Epstein. The rabbi was in his eighties and had retired. He had extensive papers (although at the time it was not realized how complete they actually were) and a storehouse of knowledge concerning almost sixty years of Atlanta and American Jewish history. His Congregation Ahavath Achim was about to celebrate its centennial the following year. Rabbi Dr. David Geffen had originally developed an extensive proposal, but his residence in Israel made completion difficult and uncertain within a finite timetable. I had done extensive work in Atlanta Jewish history and was a good friend of David, who subsequently answered my many questions. I had also worked with Jane on other projects, including an extensive 1983 exhibit commemorating 250 years of Georgia Jewish history.

After discussions with Jane, Rabbi Epstein, and Dr. William Schatten, who provided generous financial support, I agreed to undertake a series of interviews. In preparation I spoke with Mr. Cliff Kuhn, who had interviewed the rabbi and Mrs. Reva Epstein as well as many congregants, and who graciously granted me access to his recordings, transcripts, and a rough draft of a work based on these interviews. I also read extensively in the secondary literature and reviewed all of Epstein's papers. The Epstein collection, twenty-one boxes of materials, was brought to the federation for organizational purposes and subsequently given to the Jewish Community Archives of the Jewish Heritage Center housed at the federation. Not only was I afforded work space by the federation's executive director David Sarnat, but I also had the very pleasant opportunity to work with the federation's archivist, Mrs. Sandra Berman. Sandy was extremely cooperative as I read through and took notes on the materials while she processed them. She offered many insights and support, as well as several excellent suggestions after reading an early draft of this biography.

During the spring and early summer of 1986 Rabbi and Mrs. Epstein welcomed me into their home for what I am afraid became an ordeal for the rabbi, as the perhaps overzealous interviewer took many hours of the rabbi's time. I had not met the rabbi before, nor had I heard him speak except at a short wedding ceremony many years before. The series of interviews turned out to be a pure pleasure. The rabbi was gracious and forthright. His responses to my questions, on a personal level, raised questions in my mind concerning the nature of religion, ethics, and spirituality, and they helped me clarify my understanding of the various expressions of Judaism and the problems inherent in each. Copies of the tape-recorded sessions are housed at the federation archives and with the Atlanta chapter of the American Jewish Committee's Oral History Collection.

I had originally intended to compose a short article on Epstein. As my pile of notes mounted and I began to write, it became obvious that my article had turned into a book-length manuscript. The bits of information took me back into time as relationships started to appear. The image of the shtetl as a ghettoized village changed dramatically, as did the perception of Lithuanian yeshiva life. Orthodox Judaism no longer seemed so static, and Conservate Judaism made less sense to me than it had before. I started to apply insights from role theory, a helpful tool I had utilized previously for articles and a special issue of *American Jewish History*. I also found myself using categories that had been of assistance when organizing the thoughts of conservative Southern Methodist Bishop Warren A. Candler. Mark Cowitt's biography of Rabbi Morris Newfield of Birmingham raised questions about the impact of the South on a rabbi in an accommodating community, which were reinforced by the inquiries of David Geffen and others. I found relatively little regional influence on Harry Epstein. He lived a life largely prescribed by his Jewish world. Jeffrey S. Gurock has described Orthodox rabbis as either "resisters" or "accommodators" to change. Like so many others, Epstein attempted to be both. He was a pragmatist who labored to have his constituency retain as much Jewish identity as possible. With this as his primary objective for a congregation composed largely of immigrants and their children, accommodation to any peculiarly Southern norm was inconsequential. The rabbi surely interacted with the secular community and even served as an ambassador to it. Yet he was far less consumed with a desire to fit in than his Reform counterparts with their highly acculturated clientele. Thus in many respects, Epstein's experiences as a pragmatic traditionalist would have varied little had they occurred in any community of a similar nature and demography in America.

Discussions with Mrs Doris Goldstein, who was working on the centennial of Ahavath Achim and subsequently composed an illustrated history, provided many ideas, as did the very helpful comments of Professor Pamela Nadell of American University. Pamela was compiling a biographical compendium of Conservative rabbis. She graciously provided a copy of her bibliography and read and commented on a draft of my manuscript. Mrs. Bobbie S. Malone took time from her Tulane dissertation on Rabbi Max Heller to offer detailed, invaluable criticism at a late stage in the preparation of this book. Professor Sheldon Hanft of Appalachian State University asked me to deliver a paper at the Southern Jewish Historical Society meeting in Durham in November 1987. The paper, later revised and published in *American Jewish Archives* (Fall/Winter 1990), led me to reflect on the relationship between generations of immigrant subcommunities and the similarities in adjustment experiences.

Finally, I would like to thank Mr. Joseph H. Bachrach, librarian of the Saul Silber Memorial Library of the Hebrew Theological College of Chicago, and Ms. Vivian Chandler of the interlibrary loan department of Atlanta Metropolitan College library. Ms. Chandler sought out many titles I was unable to find elsewhere, and Mr. Bachrach provided much useful information on Rabbi Epstein's father and the history of the school. In addition, I would like to thank Ms. Peggy Roeske for her invaluable editorial assistance.

This volume is dedicated to my grandparents, the late Samuel and Kate Schack, Caroline Bauman, and the late Max Bauman. My maternal grandfather shortened his name from Shakhnovich shortly after coming from Russia just before World War I. Kate Steubenhaus (later shortened to Steuben) was born in New York a few years after her parents came from Austria at the turn of the century. Max Balaban changed his name to be more Americanized when he came from Czechoslovakia in the early 1920s. His wife, Caroline Islovitz, now in her sprightly nineties, a daughter and son (my father) waited several years in Europe for their departure. In 1924 immigrant restriction legislation had been passed, and my grandfather had to become a citizen prior to their admission. I think of them all with much love, warmth, and respect.

★   ★   ★

Sections of this biography appeared in slightly different form as "Rabbi Harry H. Epstein and the Adaptation of Second-Generation East European Jews in Atlanta," *American Jewish Archives* (Fall/Winter 1990): 133–46, and are used by permission of the American Jewish Archives and Managing Editor Abraham Peck.

Harry H. Epstein
and the Rabbinate
as Conduit for Change

Introduction

A major example of the process of acculturation among American Jews has been the gradual shift toward secularization, as expressed by the movement away from the traditional practice of religion. In writings about the German Jewish community during the nineteenth century, for example, the transition from "orthodoxy" to an American Reform mode of worship and belief is an obvious theme. The leaders of these seemingly opposed forces have been viewed as traditionalists versus assimilationists, or resisters juxtaposed against accommodators. From this perspective it was relatively easy to place Conservative Judaism in the pabulumlike, middle-of-the-road position. Recently, historians have come to the realization that these categories are too simplistic and do justice neither to the groups nor to the individuals involved. Each of the religious modes of expression was far more complex. Some Reform leaders wanted less change than did others, and some Orthodox spokesmen were more willing to adjust than were others. It is far more accurate to speak of a spectrum of belief and practice, and a spectrum of leadership, than of a dichotomy.[1]

Nonetheless, it is difficult for Conservative Judaism to avoid (a policy it does not necessarily desire) the centrist designation. Although what was later considered "Conservative" Judaism had its antecedents in the late nineteenth century among German Jews, it did not become a major religious alternative until it was espoused by large segments of the East European Jewish community in the decades between the world wars. Like the German Jews before them, the East Europeans gradually rose into the middle class economically and socially. They left behind "greenhorn" traits and cultural baggage, and they educated their children in the American system. For many, the old-world customs and fears slowly receded into memories, as individuals busied themselves with the opportunities offered by an open and relatively mobile environment. The children and grandchildren, lacking the memories and old-world languages,

13

could not easily associate with the necessity of maintaining the ancient religious customs in a free and voluntaristic society. Even while the immigrants required a transition involving arguments and divisions, they also were forced to deal with adaptation in order to hold their descendents within what they considered to be at least a recognizable form of Jewish worship.[2]

Harry Hyman Epstein's life spanned the twentieth century. His background and career reflect many of the important trends in American Jewish history. In many ways he was part of the themes outlined above, at the same time that he reacted to them. This biography will attempt to understand Rabbi Epstein's life and thought in historical context. This context will create a backdrop for comments on several basic themes in the American Jewish experience.

1

Lithuanian Roots

Harry Epstein's roots can be traced to two small Lithuanian towns. His father Ephraim's family was from Bakst.[1] This side of the family claimed to include a long line of rabbis. A great-great-grandfather was associated with the disciples of the Vilna Gaon, the seventeenth-century Talmudist Elijah ben Solomon Zalman. A grandfather attended the great Volozhin Yeshiva, as did his uncle. Yet not all of the family was pious. His father's generation included a labor Zionist and a businessman. Nonetheless, even these individuals absorbed the cultural orientation of the family and a love for intellectual inquiry. Unable to make a living as a rabbi, his father became a merchant in Plunge, where he married Hannah, the daughter of Israel Elijah and Leah Israelovitz. His mother's family was prosperous, her father being a successful merchant. It, too, included scholars and rabbis.

Harry was born on 1 April 1903 in Plunge. Although he left the town for America at the age of five, his memory of it was refreshed when he returned as a student in 1922. The town had but five streets, with a marketplace at its center, and it must have resembled countless similar enclaves in its region.[2]

Plunge, Bakst, and the other towns associated with Harry's stay at the Slobodka yeshiva were part of the Pale of Settlement. While there were large numbers of Jews in Poland, they had been excluded from Russia from the end of the fifteenth century through the mid eighteenth century. With the decline of the Polish Empire, the country was devoured by its more powerful neighbors in a series of partitions. In 1772, when Russia received its first slice of the Polish pie, it was confronted with the presence of the Jewish population. Nineteen years later, the czar decided to allow these Jews to help settle areas of the Black Sea recently obtained from Turkey. Jews, like other Russian ethnic groups, were limited in their mobility, but, unlike these others, they also were forbidden to trade in the Russian heartland so as not to compete with Russian merchants. During the early 1800s, as the rights of other groups slowly increased, the rights of the Jews were further proscribed. Ultimately, Russia gained additional Polish territory, including the Vilna and Grodno provinces in 1795, and extended the boundaries in which Jews could reside. Although some lands were deleted during the early nineteenth century, by 1868 the Pale of Settlement was complete and demarcated. Whereas Jews were allowed a little more mobility after this point if they came under certain classifications (e.g., students), the assassination of Alexander II in 1881 brought a sudden halt to reform and ushered in the harsh repression of government-supported pogroms.

During the early part of the twentieth century the Jewish right to settle in certain areas outside the Pale was accepted. With the onset of fighting during the First World War, Jewish refugees fled the Pale to seek safety in the Russian interior. This flight marked the de facto end of the ghettoized area. The de jure end of the Pale was granted by the Revolutionary government of 1917.

At its zenith the Pale, with a Jewish population of almost five million, extended about 386,000 square miles from the Baltic to the Black Sea. Although a little over one-tenth of the general population, in certain urbanized provinces, like Minsk, Jews representated the majority. Almost three-quarters of the Jews were employed in crafts and trade; occupations in which competition was harsh and resulted in widescale poverty. Anti-Semitism and the lack of opportunity were the key ingredients in the mass migration of these Russian/ Polish Jews to America from 1881 to World War I.

Harry Epstein's family resided in the Lithuanian area of the Russian/Polish Pale. The provinces of historic Lithuania that had become part of Poland during the fifteenth century had a character and culture of their own. Including about one and one-half million Jews by 1900, this locale was more urbanized than the rest of the Pale. The census of 1897 indicated, for example, that there were more than 212,000 Jews in the Kaunas district, slightly over 62,000 of whom resided in cities. Although the majority of the peasants were poor, the Jews largely served as businesspeople, skilled craftspeople, and merchants. They spoke their own form of Yiddish and were noted for valuing intellectual inquiry and a rational approach in opposition to emotional appeals. Within this community, culture and ideas flourished.[3]

The Jewish enlightenment, or Haskalah, entered Lithuania from Prussia, but in a particularly Lithuanian form. Its adherents, the Maskilim, accepted nationalism and a continued commitment to indigenous Jewish culture. Thus they set the foundation for modern Yiddish literature, history, and Jewish studies. The Maskilim also nurtured Russian influence among the Jews through the medium of state-supported schools and a seminary, and they contributed to the rise of Zionism and socialism among the people.

Lithuanian Jews migrated to what was then Palestine as early as the end of the eighteenth century. Settlement and nationhood were widely discussed in the local press of the 1870s. During the early years of the twentieth century, a Russian Zionist convention was held in Minsk, and a Hebrew teachers' institute opened its doors in Grodno. Lithuanian Isaac Jacob Reines was the founder of the religious Zionist Mizrachi organization.

While many Lithuanian Jews obtained relative financial success, there were many—especially at times of more overt anti-Semitic persecution—who suffered the pangs of poverty and lived the life of underpaid workers and craftsmen. The mixture of intellectual ferment and class consciousness proved to be fertile ground for socialism. In fact, Lithuania became the center of Jewish socialism and the home of the Bund. While the Bund disavowed Zionism and traditional Judaism, it fostered secular Yiddish literature and learning alongside revolution.

As secular life evolved, so, too, did religious traditionalism. Lithuania emerged as a center of Jewish scholarship, as noted commentators of the *Shulkan Arukh,* Joseph Caro's sixteenth-century compilation of Jewish law, joined its yeshivot. During the eighteenth century the apex was reached with the work of the Vilna Gaon. This master teacher emphasized intensive study of the Torah based on linguistics, knowledge of sources, and even insights into science to ascertain fundamental Talmudic meanings. In the 1800s the Gaon's followers attempted to defend their concepts against the inroads of the Haskalah, on the one hand, and Hassidism, on the other, through new yeshivot like that established by Hayyim Volozhiner in 1803. This was the yeshivot where Harry Epstein's grandfather and namesake, Zvi Hirsch Chaim, and his uncle received their rabbinic training. By the time the latter attended the Volozhin Yeshiva, however, some traditionalists realized the necessity of responding to secular appeals to Jewish youth. Led by Rabbi Israel Lipkin of Salant, these individuals added the study of Musar, or ethnics, to the yeshiva program. The reputations of the Lithuanian yeshivot grew, and they attracted brilliant students from all over Europe.

About 1863 a yeshiva was established by Zvi Levitan in Kaunas, the city the Russians called Kovno. Kovno Jews had participated in trade with Danzig (the current Gdansk) since the 1500s. They were allowed to trade intermittently and then were restricted and even expelled from the city, or murdered at the behest of their gentile competitor/neighbors. Occasionally, these Jews sought refuge in the suburb Slobodka, the site of an even older Jewish presence, where they fell under the safe umbrella of the aristocratic Radziwill family. After restrictions on settlement were removed in 1858, the Jewish community flourished. The combined population of city and suburb on the eve of the twentieth century has been estimated at twenty-five thousand, or 30 percent of the total inhabitants. Kovno became a center of Lithuanian Jewry and the home of Isaac Elhanan Spector, the Kovner Rav.[4]

In 1882, Rabbi Hirsch (Nathan) Zvi Finkel, "Der Alter," created a yeshiva stressing the Musar program, which became known as the Slobodka yeshiva. When the czar's officials closed the Volozhin yeshiva in 1892, many of its students joined Frankel's institution. The following year, as the school expanded (it ultimately had between four hundred and five hundred students), Finkel employed two brothers-in-law, Rabbis Moshe Mordecai Epstein, Harry's uncle, and Isser Zalman Meltzer.

In 1897 the yeshiva split over the issue of Musar instruction. Followers of the Salanter rabbi sought to foster the model Jewish character through piety and faith. They feared the judgment of God concerning their own imperfection and revered the pilgrim struggling with his own mission and thus easing the burden of mankind. The true Musar student, while striving to save his own soul, would help others grow in piety and knowledge to find favor with God.

Musar reflected a reaction against the legalism and tradition of those who relied on only the halachah, or law, against the rationalism of the enlightenment, and, to some extent, also against the emotionalism of Hassidism. Yet, ironically, it also was somewhat of a synthesis. Musar students would pour over texts and commentaries to derive hidden meanings in the law, strive for a purer life in faith and service, and seek out additional sources for insight and strength. The battle lines were drawn taut because the adherents of the different schools of thought viewed themselves as at the crossroads of Jewish history. Would time devoted to Musar study detract from attention to the Talmud? Could traditionalism remain relevant as Jews were exposed to a more modern world? Would the secular, modern world lead to the destructon of Jewish distinctiveness and even existence? These were some of the questions the opponents threw at each other. From their vantage point the decisions made would determine the future of a people and a religion.

Rabbis Finkel and Epstein led Knesset Israel yeshiva (named after Rabbi Lipkin and usually called the Slobodka yeshiva), and Rabbi Baruch Baer Leibowitz ran the anti-Musar Knesset Ben Yitzhak (named after Rabbi Spector). After Epstein was chosen the head rabbi of Slobodka in 1910, Finkel added his son, Moses Finkel, and his son-in-law, Isaac Sher, to the staff. By 1921, even a kollel, a graduate research institution for Talmudic studies especially for married students, was added. This was one year before Harry Epstein entered the yeshiva.

This Lithuanian milieu informed the world view of the two dominant figures in Harry Epstein's life—his father, Ephraim, and his uncle, Moshe Mordecai. Scholars, they regarded study and learning as the foundation of life. Ephraim Epstein wanted his son to enter the rabbinate, in fact, not because Harry would become the spiritual leader of a congregation, but rather so that the rabbi's role would allow and lead Harry to follow the path of lifelong learning. The mission of Ephraim and Moshe Mordecai Epstein's lives was to use their knowledge to foster the beliefs, practices, and understanding of traditional Judaism in others. This was also the righteous path to honor and prestige.[5]

Ephraim Epstein (1876–1960) was trained for the rabbinate from an early age by his father. He attended yeshiva in Slobodka where he associated with Rabbi Hirsch Finkel, the exemplar of Musar instruction. He obtained smicha (ordination) from Isaac Zalman Meltzer, the head of the Slutsk yeshiva and Moshe Mordecai's brother-in-law; the Ridbaz, Rabbi Jacob David Willovsky, commentator on the Jerusalem Talmud, chief rabbi of Slutsk and later of Chicago; Rabbi Kamai, founder of the Mir yeshiva; Yechiel Michael Epstein, author of *Aruch Hashulchan,* an outstanding legal treatise; and Rabbi Reines, founder of Mizrachi. Ephraim had been the most distinguished of Meltzer's first students. To go from rabbi to rabbi for approval and acceptance was a personal challenge and the normative fashion to test one's abilities, which Harry later emulated.

Unable to make a living in the crowded rabbinate of the area, Ephraim entered business after he married and started a family. A call from a New York congregation seemed to open new doors back into the rabbinate two decades hence. He served the New York congregation only ten months. His reputation grew, and he journeyed to Chicago, where he was asked to lead Congregation Anshe Kneseth Israel.[6]

Anshe Kneseth Israel was a substantial congregation. At the turn of the century it boasted two hundred members, twenty Torah scrolls, and a building constructed at a cost of $35,000. Originally organized in 1875 by Russian Jews as a landsleit shul (composed of people from the same area in Europe) on the west side of Chicago, it later followed its members as they migrated north. By the mid 1920s its membership totaled 450 families. It was considered one of the leading Orthodox congregations in the city, and its members were in the forefront of Jewish social service agencies.

Ephraim Epstein served the congregation from 1911 until he became senior rabbi fifty-one years later. His was a living and applied Judaism, strictly Orthodox in terms of ceremony, but capable of dealing with the world on its own terms. According to his son, Ephraim would have been happy for Orthodox rabbis even in Europe to don modern clothing if necessary to appeal to the younger generation.

He headed the Vaad Hayeshivot effort, which raised millions of dollars for aid to European yeshivot for twenty-five years during and after World War I. As a vice president of the Central Relief Committee of America and an organizer of the Relief Committee of Jewish War Sufferers, his efforts led to the formation of the Joint Distribution Committee. The rabbi attended the first American Jewish Congress in 1918, as American Jewry attempted to join hands after the war to persuade the treaty makers to accept the claims of a Jewish state. In 1946 the Joint Distribution Committee enlisted Epstein to travel through the refugee camps and to Palestine offering aid. In 1949 he again went to Israel, on this occasion to attend the first session of the Knesseth, Israel's Parliament. The rabbi served as a vice president and founder of American Mizrachi and as an officer and director of the Order Knights of Zion.[7]

Closer to home, he was a founder and vice-president of the Union of Orthodox Jewish Congregations of America and vice-president of the Agudath HaRabbanim, the Union of Orthodox Rabbis of the United States and Canada. He nurtured the creation of the Chicago Rabbinical Council. To overcome problems of Jewish educational standards, employment for Sabbath observers, and other issues, Chicago established a kehillah, or community, called the Union of Orthodox Congregations. Ephraim Epstein was, naturally, in the forefront of this movement, as he was with the Federation of Orthodox Charities. The latter, instigated by philanthropist and Sears, Roebuck president Julius Rosenwald, merged with the German Jewish charities in 1921 to form the Jewish Federation of Metropolitan Chicago. Thus the older Epstein can be viewed as bridging gaps of class and national origin to bring the Jewish subcommunities together. He helped found and served on the board of Mount Sinai Hospital, a medical center offering kosher food to its patients. All of these activities illustrate Ephraim Epstein's myriad of interests, his involvement, and the respect in which he was held by others.

No interest was closer to Ephraim Epstein's heart than Jewish education. He founded and for over thirty-five years presided over the Associated Talmud Torahs, an organization that brought order and higher standards to the often haphazard Orthodox Jewish educational efforts in Chicago. A Hebrew high school, Yeshiva Etz Chaim, had been chartered in 1899. The academic quality of this Talmud Torah was questioned by the traditionalists. To offer an alternative, three rabbis convened by Ephraim Epstein organized what became known as Beth HaMidrash LaTorah (later the Hebrew Theological College). They were probably aware of the establishment in Palestine of Chief Rabbi Kook's Merkaz ha-Rav, and of the innovative plans of the Rabbi Isaac Elchanan Theological Seminary (R.I.E.T.S.) under the new leadership of Bernard Revel. Perhaps the rabbis' actions reflected the more-pressing issue of the quality education of their own sons, and the provision of education for those in the Midwest and West who would not, or could not, go to New York. This fledgling "college" later united with Yeshiva Etz Chaim and established a teacher training institute to improve Hebrew school instruction. President of the original venture, Epstein became honorary president of the expanded enterprise. The school changed its name to the Jewish University of America in 1958 and created the Rabbi Ephraim Epstein Kollel in 1956 to commemorate the rabbi's eightieth birthday.[8]

Harry Epstein's uncle, Moshe Mordecai Epstein (1867–1933), garnered even more praise than his father. Even while a student at the Volozhin yeshiva, people referred to him as the illui, or prodigy, of Bakst. A member of Hovevei Zion (Lovers of Zion), he was deeply involved with that group's purchase of land in Haderah, Palestine, in 1891. Later, he supported Agudath Israel, an organization of Orthodox Zionists unwilling to cooperate with more secular supporters of a Jewish homeland. In 1923 he traveled to the Agudath Israel convention in Vienna, where he was elected to its executive board and its first rabbinical council. Leadership of the Slobodka yeshiva was his at the age of twenty-seven. In this capacity he fostered the "Slobodka method." This approach to the study of the Talmud emphasized planning, preparation, and the marshaling of broader knowledge into textual analysis. Each passage was studied to determine the general pattern of the legal system. It was the breadth of the methodology that distinguished it from traditional techniques.

During the First World War, when the German army occupied Slobodka, the yeshiva moved from town to town in Russia. It flourished after the war when it returned to its original site and attracted many foreign students. Lithuania emerged as an independent state in 1918 even though it remained occupied until the end of that year. Temporarily, the Jews gained substantial freedom, including government representation. Self-governing bodies were granted jurisdiction over Jewish communal affairs.

M. M. Epstein became one of the key religious leaders and a cofounder of the state rabbinical council. As Lithuania became relatively stabilized, however, it no longer felt the need to encourage its Jewish residents and reverted to the promulgation of repressive laws. Hope turned to despair, as yeshiva students lost their military exemptions and office holding was proscribed.[9]

Epstein chose ten of its best students, led by his nephew Harry, and relocated part of the yeshiva to Palestine. Some Zionist leaders had concluded that the only way to make the promises of the Balfour Declaration into reality was to expand the Jewish presence in the homeland. When Meyer Berlin, a Mizrachi founder, convinced the Palestine Executive (forerunner of the Jewish Agency) and interested individuals to fund a yeshiva, one of his critical arguments was that it was to be located in a largely Arab area. Hebron was chosen as the site in 1924. Five years hence, twenty-four students, including Harry's younger brother Aaron David, died there in a massacre.

The yeshiva again moved, this time to Jerusalem. According to an obituary later written by Harry Epstein, the Hebron slayings broke Moshe Mordecai Epstein's heart and health. Yet he continued as rosh hayeshiva (head of the yeshiva) until his death.

M. M. Epstein published a four-volume collection of lectures *(Levush Mordekhai)* clarifying Maimonides' commentaries. He read the Mishnah once every month and the Talmud once every year. His nephew recalls that during lulls in conversation he would close his eyes and mouth the portion he was studying from memory.

While scholar-activists, the Epstein brothers nonetheless were personally reserved. Harry Epstein was a student of his uncle. When the latter toured Canada and the United States to raise funds for the Hebron yeshiva in 1925–26, Harry served him as traveling companion and translator. Yet they did not seem to have spoken of personal matters, and Harry Epstein's reminiscences imply that they hardly knew each other. Even given the formality of their teacher-student relationship and the generational differences, the reserve was marked. In Slobodka and Hebron Moshe Mordecai Epstein's role was more that of an example, or a presence, to his nephew than that of a mentor, or even a teacher. The younger man sought counsel and assistance from others. To his uncle he offered respect, admiration, and even awe. The distance between them precluded the sharing of confidences and the demonstration of personal warmth.

Similar dynamics colored the father/son relationship. Ephraim Epstein countenanced neither small talk nor indulgence. Every law and custom had to be upheld absolutely within the household. According to family tradition, one should not eat lunch on Friday to heighten one's appetite for the Sabbath evening meal. Harry recalls working particularly hard one Friday morning, and, hungry from his exertions, preparing himself lunch. His father admonished him against such sinning. His father's letters, written in Yiddish and Hebrew, arrived monthly after Harry left his Chicago home. Impersonal in tone, they offered the young rabbi lessons in Talmud and suggestions for sermons. When Congregation Ahavath Achim affiliated with the Conservative movement in 1952, the father's letters stopped. A champion of Orthodoxy, Ephraim Epstein was uncompromising in his rejection of his son's direction. The son had let him and his reputation down. The Potokian flavor of the father's behavior is illustrated by other actions as well. A few years after Harry's younger brother had been killed in the Hebron massacre, the next brother in line was sent to the same yeshiva even though he showed little aptitude, or interest, in pursuing Talmudic studies.[10]

Harry Epstein learned much from these two illustrious pillars of his life. From Ephraim and Moshe Mordecai Epstein he imbibed a love of Torah and Talmud, dedication to study, and a rational approach to life. He also became a dedicated public servant, educator, and Zionist following, then elaborating on their lead.

Although he made some friends during his school years and in the rabbinate, for the most part friendships throughout his life were not close. Many of his congregants today refer to him with respect and admiration. Epstein recalls deciding against socializing with particular individuals to avoid being perceived as one who encouraged cliques. He also feared the antagonism created by having to reject certain invitations while accepting others.

Rabbi Joseph Lookstein, a contemporary, also struggled with the changing relationship between rabbi and congregants. Lookstein chose to socialize and become more accessible than the model of the East European Orthodox rabbinate; but he, too, maintained a respectful distance, and few congregants addressed him by his first name. Harry Epstein, given the examples of father and uncle, probably drew the separation even further to include rabbinic colleagues. His wife, Reva, was clearly his best friend and confidante. He best expressed his love and emotions to her.

An individual's sense of values may be identified from how he describes the good traits he perceives in others. Harry Epstein uses the terms *respect* and *honor* when describing his father and uncle. Rabbi Sher, the teacher he was closest to at the Slobodka yeshiva, he describes as a man with great faith and a lifelong student with high ethical standards. His other favorite teachers were very *dedicated*. Members of his congregation whom he respected were *charitable, intellectual,* and *learned,* willing to sacrifice for the synagogue and for others. They gained the admiration of others as they strove for excellence. Rabbi Harry Epstein hoped and assumed that he was admired and respected by his congregation. Even though certain issues caused strong disagreements with individual members, he believed that even these people respected him for his honesty and forthrightness. There is little doubt that these values were inculcated in Harry Epstein to a great extent through the examples of the two strongest role models in his life, Ephraim and Moshe Mordecai Epstein.

2

Growing Up

Harry was the oldest of nine children born to Ephraim and Hannah Epstein. A sister perished in a fire at the age of three, and a two-year-old brother was the victim of an automobile accident. Brothers Sidney and Emanuel became successful businessmen, with the latter serving as vice president of the United Synagogue of America. Harry's mother probably lived with her family in Plunge while his father established himself in America. She brought Harry and the older children with her to Chicago in 1909.[1]

Chicago was a bustling city with 75,000 Jewish residents in 1900. This population supported fifty congregations, sixty Jewish lodges, and thirty-nine Jewish charities. There were wealthy German and Polish Jews, and a multiethnic ghetto centered on Maxwell Street, which teemed with peddler and small-shop life. By 1924 the city boasted a Jewish population of three hundred thousand amid a general population of perhaps five times that number. Such a community could and did support Yiddish theater, a myriad of educational institutions, socialism, trade union associations, Zionism in various manifestations, and countless other movements and isms emanating from a dynamic American Jewry. Its streets bred both vices and opportunities.[2]

Harry Epstein's parents closely monitored his life. His father and local tutors taught him first, with the former promising ten cents for every chapter of the Bible he memorized. Later, this sum was inflated to a quarter, but Harry had to repeat the earlier chapters memorized before proceeding to (and getting rewarded for) later sections. In this way, Ephraim lured him into systematic study.

Rabbi Herman was Harry's first formal teacher of Talmud when, at the age of nine, he entered Yeshiva Etz Chaim. Rabbi Jacob Greenberg, future dean of the Hebrew Theological College, prepared him for bar mitzvah. As the need for more-advanced education arose, his father led in the organization of Beth HaMidrash HaRabbonim. While Ephraim worked to establish the school, the primary teacher was Rabbi Chaim Rubenstein. Harry traveled to Rubenstein's southside congregation, the early home of the school, to study the Talmud. Perhaps most importantly, Rubenstein imparted a love of Judaism, which reinforced Harry's home background. When Beth HaMidrash HaRabbonim moved to his father's congregation to accommodate increased enrollment, many of the students ate in his mother's kitchen.

Harry described himself and the other thirteen- and fourteen-year-olds who studied with him as "five wild animals" who only thought about playing baseball. He had played third base for his elementary school softball squad and liked to peek through the Wrigley Field fences with his friends to see Chicago Cubs games. Still, Harry gained much from his rather peripatetic secular education. His eighth-grade teacher exposed him to opera, and Dr. McLean, a tenth-grade instructor, fostered an enduring love for history. The Latin Harry took from Mrs. Zimmerman further expanded his outlook. Harry became the play-maker guard of the Marshall High School basketball team.

In his study of Yeshiva University, Jeffrey S. Gurock brings out the conflict Orthodox parents and educators had in New York City struggling with the relationship between secular studies and yeshiva preparation. Although staunchly traditional in appearance, in a comparative sense the Epsteins took the moderate approach to their son's upbringing. The public school was the primary educational vehicle during the day, and religious instruction was relegated to the afternoons.[3]

Nonetheless, at Beth HaMidrash HaRabbonim, Harry's teachers prepared him for the best Orthodox training then available in America. Ephraim Epstein apparently also recognized the limits of his school and wanted his son to have a broad-based background. Thus, Harry was sent to New York to attend the Rabbi Isaac Elchanan Theological Seminary. East European immigrants with the support of their more-established brethren had established this seminary, named for Rabbi Spector of Kovno, in 1897 to train Orthodox rabbis. Conflict frequently marked its path. While the old guard wanted it to retain the traditional approach to learning, the newer generation and students advocated secular studies alongside rabbinics, and professional training integrated with Talmudics.

With the selection of Bernard Revel to head the school in 1915, the accommodationists claimed temporary victory. Until his death in 1940, with the exception of a short interlude to take care of family business, Revel presided over the school, which became the foundation of Yeshiva University. He was a dreamer with a vision of how American Jewry would be called on to lead world Jewry. When he taught Harry Epstein, the young student came to think of him as "personally my rabbi." Consciously or unconsciously, the older man challenged his protégé to act independently. Epstein shared Revel's dreams while opposing the application of certain policies.[4]

Revel's pride in America informed his desire to have American rabbinical students trained in America as opposed to Europe. Yet R.I.E.T.S., as his yeshiva was called, could only confer a Yoreh Yoreh ("he will teach, he will teach") ordination and not the advanced Yadin Yadin ("he will judge, he will judge") confirmation of rabbinic expertise. A brilliant student, Harry Epstein was encouraged to pursue his studies in Lithuania by his teachers, at least according to his memory. In fact, Epstein attended R.I.E.T.S. during a critical period of the school's history, while Revel spent much of his time in Tulsa attempting to rejuvenate his in-law's oil business. The school suffered from a lack of leadership and continued debate over the relationship between secular and religious studies, and between homiletics and Talmudics. These factors also may have influenced the decision.

Yet, prior to his return to Slobodka, the surprising decision was made for him to attend the University of Chicago. The classes at the university were very large. Epstein studied philosophy under Professor Aimes and German under Deutsch. He viewed the archaeological exhibits prepared by renowned Egyptologist J. H. Breasted and attended a lecture presented by visiting Albert Einstein. In 1921, Chicago was considered a hotbed of theological modernism, with its emphasis on biblical criticism and secular rationalism.[5] Although Harry Epstein was greatly influenced by these forces, he was an eighteen-year-old undergraduate at this time. It is questionable how much this stay and another on his return from Hebron directly impacted on his later thought.

What is apparent, however, is that Harry Epstein was being exposed to a highly eclectic education, and the choices were probably being made by his father. In the last decade the stereotypical image of monolithic Orthodox intransigence has been effectively demol-

ished by Jeffrey S. Gurock, Aaron Rothkoff, Louis Bernstein, Jenna
W. Joselit, and others. From these historians has come a picture of
substantial internal division and variation over observance, philosophy, and especially education. Disputes over the supervision of ritual
slaughter, relations with Conservatives and Reformers, and attitudes
toward the establishment of a Jewish state were the norm.[6]

Given the image Harry Epstein maintained of his father and uncle
and the knowledge available concerning their backgrounds and associations, it would be logical to include them among the most strin-
gently and uncompromisingly Orthodox. Yet, his uncle frowned on
secular studies and would have only begrudgingly allowed a minimal
number of secular classes after the completion of a day of traditional
Talmudic discourse. To these people, even the Rabbi Isaac Elchanan
Theological Seminary was somewhat suspect and had to be kept
under constant surveillance.

On the inverse of this equation were a growing number of American Orthodox rabbis who recognized the need for secular education
of the highest caliber to complement traditional study. These individuals realized that the East European immigrants were achieving,
like Ephraim Epstein's Chicago congregants, levels of middle- and
upper-class success. The lay rise in status fueled their desire for rabbis
who could associate with the gentile community, a process similar
to that which the German Jews underwent fifty years before. Even
more critically for the Eastern Europeans in the interwar years, their
children were obtaining fine college educations. The American identity of the second generation equaled, or surpassed, their association
as Jews. To communicate with them, the rabbi would have to be a
capable, well-educated, and well-rounded English speaker who could
present sermons informed on secular as well as religious questions.

As witnessed by the education he designed for his son, Ephraim
Epstein, a leader of the resistant-to-change Union of Orthodox Rabbis of America and Canada, tacitly accepted what many in the 1920s
perceived as these inevitable accommodations. During this same decade graduates of the Hebrew Theological College of Chicago accepted pulpits in Midwestern congregations with mixed seating.
This trend was widely viewed as a key step toward Conservatism.
With a bit of sophistry, the college refrained from disowning these
alumni on the grounds that they might lead the congregations back
to the Orthodox path of separation of the sexes during services.
There is no record of Ephraim Epstein's opposition to this position.

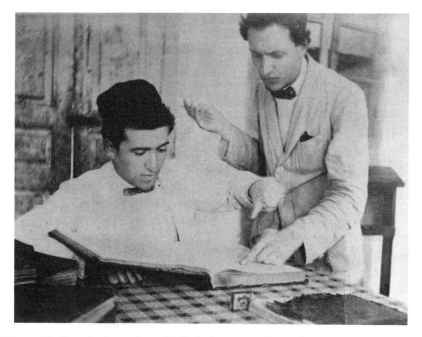

Harry H. Epstein (seated) and Yitchak Vetker, his study partner and friend. Hebron Yeshiva, Palestine, ca. 1925. Reproduced by permission of Atlanta Jewish Heritage Center and Rabbi Harry H. Epstein.

One can only conjecture that the father, like many of his generation and like his son later, struggled with the problem of where to draw the line on change. He desired one reality but saw another.

Harry Epstein, with an education comparable to his contemporaries Leo Jung and Joseph Lookstein, was being prepared to bridge the gap between the first and second generations, and to keep the latter as much within the fold as possible. A return to the roots in Lithuania and the scholarship its yeshivas constituted offered entrée to the old guard and was the necessary ingredient for the father's compromise.

When the young scholar went to his uncle's Slobodka yeshiva in 1922, the school was in its prime. Located in a suburb of the capital with "old fashioned, decaying wooden houses," it held 400 students in a two-story building. A relatively independent Lithuania opening opportunities for Jews in business and government attracted some of the world's best Talmudic minds. Most of the learning was based on independent study and exchange between students. An extant picture in the Epstein scrapbooks from latter days in Hebron has Harry posed with a study mate, both dressed in coats and bow ties, pointing to a passage in an open text in mock debate. Another picture illustrates students seated with lecturnlike desks tilted toward them as they read. Rabbi Epstein holds the fondest memories for the dynamic and brilliant students. He brought one of these, Herzl Kaplan, back to America with him after completion of their studies, and he recommended him for a position at the Hebrew Theological College, which Kaplan ultimately filled with distinction.[7]

Although the five different heads of the yeshiva lectured from noon to one or one-thirty daily, the more intimate contacts and the philosophies to which Harry Epstein was exposed seem to have had the more lasting impact. From his uncle he garnered an image of the scholar devoted to learning. Moshe Mordecai Epstein could enter into extremely lengthy and detailed discussions of the Talmud in an attempt to resolve apparent contradictions. Harry Epstein had a closer relationship with Rabbi Finkel, who taught him the ethical basis of Judaism through the study of Musar. Finkel's emphasis was on mystical faith in the sight of God and humanity.

Rabbi Isaac Sher, who assumed control of the yeshiva in Slobodka when part of the institution was relocated in Palestine and who headed the school into the Holocaust years, became Harry's personal tutor and confidant. The youth met with his tutor once each week, in part to facilitate the adjustment of an American to Lithuanian yeshiva life. Of Sher, Epstein asked a pivotal question in Judaism and in the latter's life. If the two most-important commandments were to love God and to love thy neighbor as thyself, is it possible to teach others to have faith and to love God and humanity? Sher's answer, adapted from the teachings of Judah Ha-Levi and of Hillel— that you might not necessarily love another, but that you should not do something to another that you would not want that person to do to you—never satisfied Epstein. The question haunted him then, led to his choice of a master's thesis topic, and continued to puzzle him throughout his life.

For an understanding of Epstein's philosophical maturation, it is necessary to view the Slobodka yeshiva as a culmination of the ideas flowing through Lithuania in the nineteenth and early-twentieth centuries. The yeshiva exposed him to mysticism and rationalism, Talmudic literalism, and an ethical commitment to service. The students wore modern clothing and shaved their faces. However,

Harry H. Epstein (standing) and Yitchak Vetker. Jerusalem, ca. 1925. Reproduced by permission of Atlanta Jewish Heritage Center and Rabbi Harry H. Epstein.

Harry H. Epstein and Rabbinic tutor. Slobodka Yeshiva, Lithuania, ca. 1924. Reproduced by permission of Atlanta Jewish Heritage Center and Rabbi Harry H. Epstein.

with Harry as an exception (another concession to his American upbringing), the pursuit of secular learning, the reading of newspapers, and the direct study of the Bible were forbidden. The Haskalah, or Jewish enlightenment, was anathema to M. M. Epstein.

Nevertheless, it was difficult to limit such earnest thinkers to the traditional codes and commentaries. Although the training prepared one for the shtetl life of the Talmudist, it could also lead to critical analysis and broader horizons. For a Harry Epstein, it opened the path to biblical exegesis, a rational approach to modernizing the practice of Judaism and to studying Jewish thought, and a respect for those who sought insights into the fundamentals of Judaism from different perspectives. Acceptance of given law and belief based on faith intertwined and juxtaposed with enlightened skepticism probably left the student with a brilliant background and with more questions than answers.

Harry Epstein was one of the ten students chosen to go to Hebron with his uncle to establish a branch of the yeshiva in Palestine, probably based on his academic promise, dedication, and ability to adjust. He traveled by ship from Europe to Egypt, and from there by train to his destination. Harry Epstein's two years in Hebron, an Arab-dominated city, were the loneliest of his life. The yeshiva and the community did not mix. Friendships had to be from within. The attitudes of the European students did not help. They separated from, and considered themselves superior to the Americans. Epstein recalls being an exception to this separation, as a brilliant scholar whom they respected, but this reflection is over a half century later. Possibly, these experiences reinforced his tendencies to remain removed from intimate friendships and contributed to his later Zionism and absorption in ethnic affairs. He enjoyed the unusual distinction of receiving the parchment smicha and baccalaureate degree simultaneously.

For smicha, or ordination, the certification of three rabbis was required. The process tested the individual's ability, offered role models, and provided a source of continued pride. Sometimes, short discussions testing one's knowledge sufficed. Other rabbis expected longer encounters for a more thorough testing and to exert their intellectual, or moral, influence. One could point to the testimonials smicha implied, claiming status and prestige professionally, for example, when applying for positions. The lure of the highest accep-

Hebron Yeshiva, Palestine, ca. 1924. Reproduced by permission of Atlanta Jewish Heritage Center and Rabbi Harry H. Epstein.

tance from esteemed rabbinic authorities challenged the youth further.

Recognition from five other rabbis served as a prerequisite for smicha from the chief rabbi. After his uncle, Epstein sought out the second leading rabbi in the Holy Land. Yaacov Moshe Charlap was a saintly man steeped in Musar, who, according to Epstein, never ventured out of Jerusalem a day in his entire life. Harry spent a month with him taking daily walks. When he journeyed to Israel for a sabbatical half a century later, he made a special pilgrimage to Charlap's small shul, Zichrono livracha. Other certificates came from Rabbi Yechiel Epstein of the Torat Chaim Yeshiva, from the Teblik rabbi, and from a Rabbi Auerbach of the Shar Shemayim yeshiva. Harry Epstein was now ready for Rabbi Abraham Isaac Kook.[8]

Harry thought of Kook as "the most unusual person of the century." Kook stood for the pioneers, the common people of Palestine. He saw "no evil in any man." His mind would drift as if in mystical reverie when contemplating people, God, and the possibilities for

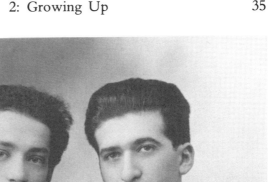

Harry H. Epstein (right) and Herzl Kaplan at the time of their smicha (ordination). Jerusalem, 1926. Reproduced by permission of Atlanta Jewish Heritage Center and Rabbi Harry H. Epstein.

the future. Born in Latvia, Kook mixed the traditional Talmudic education with study of the Bible, Hebrew, philosophy, and mysticism. After moving to Jaffa in 1904, he gained a reputation for bringing together individuals of different opinion. Attending an Agudath Israel convention a decade later, he was forced to remain in Europe for the duration of World War I. After the war, he became chief rabbi first of Jerusalem and then of all Palestine. His concept of Zionism encompassed not only the revival of a Jewish homeland but also the spiritual-redemptive aspects of a broadly Jewish renewal. In terms of yeshiva education, this master of the Merkaz ha-Rav emphasized the mixture of secular and clerical learning. His students were well trained as authors and lecturers so that they could reach out to their modern audiences. In Kook's thought the modern mind had to treat the concepts of the larger human community, and religion had to be reconciled with science and especially evolution. To keep youth within Judaism and to make Judaism relevant to contemporary life, he emphasized social justice and merged secular and ecclesiastical concerns.[9]

Rabbi Kook's thought clearly presaged that of Rabbi Harry Epstein. In fact, the younger man's positions were a mirror of those of this scholar/activist. Yet, it is most difficult to gauge the impact of a short, albeit direct contact, even during someone's formative years. More likely, a synthesis evolved. Epstein was influenced by the contact with Kook and with teachers and scholars who had either been influenced by Kook, or who had drawn the same conclusions independently. Epstein also observed the same situations, made the same observations, and came to the same conclusions.

Having received this ultimate smicha and overcome another challenge, Harry Epstein returned to America. He attended a few more terms at the University of Chicago without completing the requirements for a degree. Although his father had earlier convinced him to pursue a career in the rabbinate instead of medicine, the older man wanted to further guide his son. Ephraim Epstein made him bide his time by informing him only of the least-desirable rabbinical vacancies.

When Moshe Mordecai Epstein came to America to raise funds for his yeshiva in 1926, Harry was enlisted to travel with his uncle and to act as his English spokesman. The young man demurred that his only public speaking experience had occurred at his bar mitzvah. This objection disclosed another anomaly in his education. A series of student strikes and protests had influenced the Rabbi Isaac Elchanon Theological Seminary trustees to institute courses in homiletics. These classes trained the young men in the practical aspects of rabbinical careers, including the preparation and delivery of sermons. Because he left R.I.E.T.S. for Europe, Epstein had never shared these opportunities. His destiny did not rest in his own hands.

Harry Epstein spent nine months traveling with his uncle from Montreal to New York, Washington, Memphis, and Dallas and on to California, and writing articles treating his yeshiva years for the Jewish press. He had the time of his life.[10] His natural speaking acumen in Yiddish and English and his fund-raising ability did not go unnoticed. Congregation B'nai Emunah of Tulsa offered him the position as its spiritual leader. He served this Oklahoma congregation for a year before obtaining a similar post in Atlanta.

His rabbinical duties did not deter him from fulfilling his father's educational mandate and his own thirst for improvement. From 1929 through 1932 he took courses at Emory University leading to the granting of a Bachelor of Philosophy degree and a Master of Arts degree in theology. He attended classes in education, philosophy, biology, English, and history. His surviving term papers reflect the work of a mature individual planning his studies around career objectives. He pursued his interest in mysticism in a study of Maurice Maeterlinck's *The Blue Bird* for an English professor, and he conducted research on cabala for a course on that subject. For biology, he wrote about the philosophy of evolution. Other paper topics included the philosophy of values, Aristotlean ethics, and Arab contributions to European thought. Epstein was comparing and contrasting Jewish learning and thought with those of other civilizations and, in the process, identifying the sources of Judaism and the core beliefs of religion. This approach was unheard of within the traditional yeshiva context in which the Talmud and commentaries would have been considered self-sufficient for such questions. Epstein was educating himself within the new mold and making himself more of a universalist. His grades were uniformly high, and his bibliographies reflected substantial research. The knowledge he gained was reflected in his sermons and in his master's thesis, which was a preliminary investigation of the different ways in which Jewish schools of thought tried to determine certainty.[11] Rabbi Epstein's search for ideas took him outside the narrow confines of the pulpit to continue his personal search for growth. An unidentified reader of his thesis commented, "Mr. Epstein's problem has the merit of having arisen out of his own perplexities as an interpreter of Jewish Orthodoxy."[12] To answer the questions he had asked of Rabbi Sher, he took a path through secular studies.

Emory's professors seemed to have taken a special interest in this clearly unusual and advanced student. Wyatt A. Smart, the theology school dean of this Methodist-associated university, called on the rabbi to speak at chapel services. Thomas English had him conduct English classes, and Woolfolk B. Baker later wrote with pride of the accomplishments of his biology student. Epstein most appreciated his thesis advisor. Leroy E. Loemke had worked his way through school as a Pullman car conductor. Although intellectually stimulating to the rabbi, when the professor gave a lecture as requested at Congregation Ahavath Achim, Epstein feared that the talk was beyond the audience's level of comprehension.[13]

Through the 1940s and into the 1950s, Epstein was asked to give lectures in Bible classes and to speak before different Christian student forums. He was a logical individual to lead in the formation of a Hillel chapter on campus in 1947. He respected the Emory community, and it returned his admiration.

In 1952, as he entered the twenty-fifth year in the Ahavath Achim pulpit, and the year the congregation affiliated with the Conservative movement, Harry Epstein earned the Doctor of Philosophy degree and took correspondence courses in the pursuit of a Doctor of Theology degree. The University of Illinois School of Law allowed him to study in Atlanta and take examinations in Illinois to complete the requirements for a doctorate. The Central School of Religion in Indiana had a more demanding program in which the rabbi was engaged in directed correspondence courses. These courses required extensive reading and lengthy research reports. Although he chose classes in marriage and the family, the philosophy of education, and social psychology, the stress was clearly on comparative religion and ancient philosophy. He continued to specialize in the Greeks as he explored the relationship between Socrates and Aristotle and the Jewish outlook on life. A Church of Christ pastor/instructor commented that Epstein's report for a comparative religion course was the best he had ever received. Another professor suggested that Epstein prepare his own courses and become a teacher for the program.

Whereas this study completed Harry Epstein's formal education, he also was awarded a Doctor of Divinity degree at the eightieth anniversary of the Jewish Theological Seminary in 1966. He was one of eighty and the only rabbi from the South so honored.[14]

As his father had wished, Harry Epstein pursued a life of learning. Having completed one of the best courses of Talmudic study available, he followed contemporary American practice in obtaining a sound secular education as well. The frequent references in speeches and sermons to works on history, literature, religion, and philosophy and the frequent book review classes he conducted provide evidence of Epstein's lifelong informal study. While the rabbinate was conducive to the continuing quest for understanding, that quest, in turn, offered an outstanding foundation for a successful rabbinical career.

3

The First Full-Time Pulpit

When Harry Epstein was elected spiritual leader of Tulsa's Congregation B'nai Emunah, having been victorious over ten other applicants, he was an extremely well-prepared twenty-four year-old.[1] The year of travel, speaking, and writing with his uncle in behalf of the Hebron yeshiva crowned a superior education. His family background was another major contributing factor to his maturity. The maturity, evident in his early sermons and the articles he composed for the local newspapers, was more than a personal attribute. Here was a man who had a well-defined view of the role of the modern Orthodox rabbi, understood the needs of the Jewish community of the 1920s, and knew what he wanted to accomplish.

The rabbi would first be a teacher and build a sense of Jewishness among the congregation's members. Epstein's motto for his ministry early became "Neither a reformed synagogue, nor a deformed synagogue, but an informed synagogue." To him this meant, in part, that he would attempt to inculcate knowledge and a deeper love of Judaism to create a climate that would nurture greater and more meaningful observance. He would teach Zionism as an integral aspect of Judaism, and would encourage participation in the congregation and in community social services. He also would reach out to the Christian community as he taught the meaning of Musar through example. To those who asked, "why need we conform at present with faith? In Moses' time it was necessary, but not now," Epstein responded, holding with the thought of Leopold Zunz, that a "Progressive Judaism [would be a] Judaism in accordance with the times." For this, faith and the practical application of that faith were still essential.[2]

Tulsa's was an old, established congregation. To fit the image of his and the membership's expectations, Harry Epstein grew a mustache. He also decided to define his position at the onset of his tenure.

His first sermon was entitled "Studies in Leadership." He spoke of the kings of ancient Israel from the Sabbath text and concluded that the contemporary rabbis had now assumed the mantel of leadership. The qualities he outlined for the capable leader were spirituality and dedication to the people's needs. The rabbi had to be a supporter of the traditions and a promulgator of Judaism. He "must take up the banner of the traditions of the faith. He must carry aloft the flag of our culture, and with his imbued fire of spirituality, he must lead his people . . . to loftier scopes of morality and divinity. Truly a rabbi is one of the community, ordained and authorized to teach, guide and enlighten his people, his comrades, to show them a nobler path in life." The rabbi was one with his people, but yet above them "when it is his duty and responsibility to proclaim dauntlessly and fearlessly the word of God, the principle of religion, the rule of humanity and the admonitions of the law."

The following year Epstein enlarged on this model with his installation sermon at Congregation Ahavath Achim. On this occasion he again related the role of the rabbi to that of the biblical kings, and this time also to that of the priests. These leaders could be friendly, peaceful, and compassionate, but also righteous prophets denouncing shortcomings.[3]

Such role images could be difficult burdens to bear, especially for one's first pulpit. The Oklahoma congregation posed special challenges because of the nature of the membership and because of personal connections. The congregation president, David Travis, was Bernard Revel's brother-in-law. Revel had not wanted Epstein to go to Slobodka and considered the Tulsa congregation to be his province. Epstein again warmed to the opportunity of testing his mettle. While Rabbi Epstein probably succeeded in the second test, he ultimately rejected the first. The congregation was wealthy and dominated by older figures. The oil magnates routinely asked him to pray for the success of their wells. Conflicts between individual congregants resulted in both going to the young rabbi and urging him to ignore the other. Both sides volunteered to guarantee his salary. While he denounced materialism from the pulpit and in articles published in the local newspapers, this environment was not to his liking. He felt more like a puppet or a plaything than one who was needed or wanted for spiritual guidance.[4]

Rabbi Harry H. Epstein. Tulsa, Okla., 1927. Reproduced by permission of Atlanta Jewish Heritage Center and Rabbi Harry H. Epstein.

Still, Harry Epstein viewed his year in Tulsa as a learning experience. He met with President Travis every Monday morning at ten to determine which charities the latter would contribute to for the week. Few requests were rejected. Mr. Livingston, a retired oil magnate, studied the Talmud constantly and showed Epstein still another example of an individual imbued with a love for learning. Another scholar wrote an English commentary on the Book of Job. Finally, Epstein was inducted into the Masonic fellowship while in Tulsa. He later joined the Shrine after achieving the thirty-second degree in the Scottish Rite. He became an expert in "the ancient rites and ceremonies" of the Masonic Lodge of Sorrow, gaining the authority to conduct the funeral service. Epstein considered Masonry to be "a wonderful training ground for everything we in the religious field try to inculcate in the minds of our followers."[5] Learning early to become a "joiner," he recognized the benefits of extended contacts and personal involvement in community affairs.

While he was in Tulsa, Harry Epstein's reputation as an exemplar of the modern Orthodox rabbinate started to grow. This reputation brought him to the attention of Atlanta's Congregation Ahavath Achim, which next sought and obtained his services.

4

Ahavath Achim and Modern Orthodoxy

Congregation Ahavath Achim had been established by East European Jews in 1887. These Jews had not felt comfortable in the German Jewish Hebrew Benevolent Congregation ("The Temple"), which was moving in the direction of Reform. The creation of the new congregation represented basic divisions educationally, culturally, and economically between the two groups as well as in their relative levels of acculturation. The two subcommunities were different and were unwilling to accept each other. Yet, as the East European Jewish community of Atlanta grew and changed, it, too, became differentiated. Twenty years hence second and third East European Orthodox congregations opened their doors.[1]

By the early twentieth century, more than two decades had passed since the first East European Jews had arrived. These people had moved up economically, learned English, and started to work on a more equitable basis with the German Jews, especially through the Federation of Jewish Charities and organizations like B'nai B'rith. They represented what sociologist Marshall Sklare has described as the second area of settlement, one ripe for the introduction of Conservatism. Their children were clearly Americanized as they passed through the public school system and entered college, business, and the professions.

Part of the process of Americanization for the first generation was represented by the creation of Congregation Beth Israel, a decade-long attempt at "conservative" Judaism. The leaders of this Ahavath Achim offshoot included many economically successful former presidents of the parent body. They employed very capable young rabbis fluent in English and deeply committed to Zionism and the community. This congregation came very close to being accepted by The Temple crowd, but it was ultimately thwarted by the hostility of Ahavath Achim. Small in terms of members, it was unable to keep its rabbis for any length of time. Although a few members refused reconciliation with the old congregation out of a sense of pride and resentment and some joined The Temple, most returned to Ahavath Achim. As these individuals rejoined, they could not help but bring a desire for change with them. Into the 1920s this group increased in number, particularly as their children—lacking the European Jewish background and imperative—either stopped attending or followed the forms without the substance of religious practice. Still, even after the start of Shearith Israel in 1902—a more traditional Orthodox congregation of newer immigrants who were typically poorer and less acculturated—a sizable segment of Ahavath Achim's membership consisted of resisters to accommodation.[2]

These problems were frequently compounded with the presence of an older generation of European-born and -trained rabbis. Many of these rabbis lived in America but continued to think in old world patterns. They rejected accommodation and urged their congregants to live by the letter of the law. Rather than adjust, they seemingly wanted the environment to accommodate their way of life. Shearith Israel's Tobias Geffen exemplified this role, as did Ahavath Achim's Abraham P. Hirmes.

The scanty extant evidence indicates that Hirmes was born in Lithuania and trained at the Slobodka yeshiva and at the Rabbi Isaac Elchanan Theological Seminary. He came to America about 1900 and was thirty-six years old when he became the rabbi of the congregation in 1919. Hirmes felt more comfortable speaking his native Yiddish and holding Talmudic study sessions with older congregants than trying to communicate with younger, or more-acculturated older, members in his halting English. Services rambled and lacked a sense of decorum. Although Hirmes led a United Hebrew School, the religious educational level of the students left much to be desired. Lay leaders of the old guard held sway. Joel Dorfan, who presided over the congregation for twenty-eight years, including the Hirmes decade (not an uncommon occurence in Orthodox synagogues throughout the country during this era), gave "sermons" based on his reading of the Jewish newspapers and then asked the rabbi if he had anything to add. The less-atuned spiritual leader usually did not. Little is recorded concerning Hirmes's departure in 1928, even before Epstein's arrival. It seems likely that the decision may have been mutual. Certainly from the congregation's perspective, under

Hirmes it was at best treading water and, more realistically, languishing into decline.[3]

Thus, during the decade between the world wars, Ahavath Achim was confronted with a series of interrelated dilemmas. How could one congregation meet the needs of apparently different and competing constituencies? Regardless of which direction the congregation took, segments of its population would react negatively. In larger communities capable of supporting numerous organizations, synagogues broke asunder, continued with reduced membership, or multiplied. Moreover, membership declined as people moved away from the old neighborhoods, sought their Jewish identity through participation in Jewish clubs and organizations, or simply ended formal association altogether. In communities the size and nature of Atlanta, where the multiplication of synagogues beyond a modest number was impractical, the burden was even greater for those who sought the continuation and growth of active synagogue affiliation.

Ahavath Achim's situation was more typical than unique. The German Jewish community had experienced a similar juncture a half century earlier. As David Ellenson has shown, the Orthodox leadership responded in a variety of ways. Those like Rabbi Seligman Baer Bamberger, dug in their heels, refused to accept any sort of change, and even rejected recognition of any other expressions of Judaism.

Samson Raphael Hirsch also responded to the challenges posed to traditional Judaism by the lure of Reform and the forces of modernism by emphasizing the separatism and distinctiveness of Judaism and the hallowing of tradition. Yet, Hirsch defended his position from the Western cultural matrix. Armed with a doctorate from a German university besides the requisite yeshiva imprimatur, Hirsch used German language and philosophical thought to buttress his arguments. His mode of expression appealed to enlightened, worldly Jews who nonetheless wanted to retain the Jewish religious way of life.

Esriel Hildesheimer tried to bridge the gap in the Orthodox response. While defending the immutability of the law and the authority of the rabbi like his two contemporaries, Hildesheimer respected and utilized German norms, but, to an extent contrasting with Hirsch, he also thought, spoke, and wrote in Yiddish and Hebrew modes.

Although all three rabbis refused to cooperate with Reform Jews on religious matters, Hirsch and Hildesheimer cooperated with them and even with non-Jews in philanthropic endeavors. Moreover, they accommodated through flexibility in what they defined as non-fundamental ceremonial customs.[4]

The distinctions between Bamberger, Hirsch, and Hildesheimer were highly significant for their congregants. Language and form served as symbols with deep emotional content for those grappling with the age-old struggle between continuity and change. Traditional yeshiva education and ordination, the use of Yiddish and Hebrew, in discourse and writing, resort to responsa (essays clarifying legal questions based on the Torah and commentaries), auctioning ceremonial honors like recitation of the prayers before and after the reading of the Torah to the highest bidders during services, or men chanting prayers at their own pace during services were the comfortable and usual ways of doing things that had evolved over hundreds of years. Rabbis with doctorates from secular universities who spoke and wrote in the vernacular, vernacular sermons, orderly services with control over behavior and decorum, acquiescence in a pluralistic society and cooperation with people with divergent religious beliefs and practices, and attempts to explain theory and practice to congregants who had formerly accepted faith and authority served as benchmarks for innovation. People argued these points, and congregations divided over them. Reform and traditional rabbis and lay people accepted and rejected various outward signs as they accepted varying degrees of acculturation. Reform had created an ideological justification for change, which, during the nineteenth century, ultimately undercut substantial amounts of customary practice. Many who would conserve tradition opposed the fundamental changes the Reform ideas implied even as they felt the necessity to accept certain outward symbols of adjustment.

Bamberger, Hirsch, and Hildesheimer had their counterparts in the United States. During the nineteenth century the first ordained rabbi in America, Abraham Rice, played the Bamberger part. Unordained and only informally trained, Isaac Leeser accepted Hirsch's role. Both supported Orthodoxy and opposed Reform. But, while Rice was uncompromising, Leeser developed educational materials and tools of communication, including a newspaper in English, altered certain religious practices to appeal to American traditional Jews, and sought common ground with Isaac M. Wise, the institution builder of American Reform.[5]

Late in the century, Hirsch's American colleagues propounded what became known as neo-Orthodoxy. In 1886 they founded the Jewish Theological Seminary (J.T.S.) in reaction to Reform's Pittsburgh Platform of beliefs, and the Association of American Orthodox Hebrew Congregations to counteract Wise's Union of American Hebrew Congregations. Led by Rabbis Bernard Drachman and Henry Pereira Mendes among others, they wanted to mediate between the demands of American and Jewish culture to keep Jews within the fold. They modernized education, compromised Sabbath observance, used the English language for prayers, and brought dignity to the service. When the J.T.S. veered too much toward Conservative Judaism under Solomon Schechter, and the Rabbi Isaac Elchanan Theological Seminary merged with yeshiva Etz Chaim in 1915 to form the Rabbinical College of America with Bernard Revel as its president, they looked to this new school to train American-born rabbis in Talmudic, biblical and secular studies (the last were to be obtained from neighboring institutions). Their sense of urgency was heightened in the 1920s as Conservative Judaism enticed a growing number of second-generation immigrant children.

Rabbis Joseph Lookstein and Leo Jung exemplified the modern Orthodox approach in the interwar years, and their experiences and careers approximated those of Harry Epstein. The much better known Lookstein and Jung from the leadership base of New York, like Epstein in the regional nexus of Atlanta, promoted what Jenna Weissman Joselit has aptly termed a "cultured," or "reasonable," Orthodoxy to moderate the American influence on an emergent middle-class Jewry. Lookstein, born in Russia, came to the United States in 1912 at the age of twelve. He attended R.I.E.T.S. and received a master's degree from City College of New York. Jung, a decade older and born in Moravia, graduated from Hildesheimer's seminary and obtained the doctorate from Cambridge University. Lookstein gained the acceptance of the old guard by serving as Moses Z. Margolies's (the RAMAZ) English-speaking assistant at Kehilath Jeshurun and marrying his granddaughter. He dressed and spoke like a dignified modern rabbi. Borrowing the model of decorum and scholarship from his Reform peers, Lookstein provided his congregants with a modern education in Orthodox beliefs while sidestepping laxity in personal practices outside of the synagogue. Jung, whom Joselit calls the "epitome of orthodoxy," supervised the Jewish Center for sixty-five years, and he nurtured a scholarly foundation for modern Orthodoxy based on ethics, aesthetics, and patriotism. In practice, he, like Lookstein and Epstein, made the synagogue a social setting compatible with middle-class family life. Seeking advice from the old guard, Rabbi Jung blended European cultural Orthodoxy with urbanity. Jung and Lookstein felt comfortable lecturing in the college classroom, volunteering for interdenominational social service causes, and speaking on the radio. Theirs was a traditional Judaism from which their congregants gained pride and comfort.

These modern Orthodox spokesmen compromised what they defined as nonessential customs in order to maintain the essence of the laws. They viewed Judaism as a religion evolving through the guidance of the learned rabbi. Their ideas reflected the same tendencies as Europe's Zacharias Frankel, who saw history as continuing revelation, and American contemporary Mordecai Kaplan's perception of Judaism as an adapting culture. Yet, Frankel and Kaplan are frequently seen as influential figures in the rise and development of Conservative Judaism. Herein lay one of the key conundrums for modern Orthodox practitioners. Once they started on the road to compromise and maintained membership through adjustment, they blurred the demarcation between Orthodoxy and the increasingly attractive Conservative alternative. According to Joselit, in the post–World War II era, when their legitimacy was challenged by a new wave of European Orthodox and ethnic distinctiveness allowed for an Orthodox revival, the Jewish expression of Lookstein and Jung appeared denatured and irrelevant. Epstein, who took his congregation almost inexorably into Conservative affiliation, experienced the same frustrations and doubts.

In the early and mid 1920s the lines of disagreement and organizational conflict were not always so apparent, nor was the potential opening of the Conservative door. Seeming inconsistencies, for example, in Ephraim Epstein's theory and practice previously identified can be addended. Rabbis Lookstein, Jung, David De Sola Pool, and their allies formed the Rabbinical Council of America in 1935, in part, to counteract the activities of the Agudath HaRabbonim, Ephraim's rejectionist rabbinical agency. Epstein's Hebrew Theological College alumni association incorporated into the Council. Joseph Lookstein spoke at Ephraim Epstein's eightieth birthday celebration in 1956 on the topic "New Path for Old Tradition." Turmoil, variety, and irony clearly epitomized twentieth-century Orthodoxy.

Ahavath Achim's membership may or may not have been aware of these patterns. They were aware of a need for an alternative to Rabbi Hirmes. Their choice seemed to be between moving forward and expanding, and stagnation and decline. The young Rabbi Harry Epstein, as had Jung and Lookstein, realized that change would also have to reflect continuity. He would win over the traditionalists first and introduce innovation at a slower pace than that desired by the younger members to shore up his authority. Epstein recalls losing some of the latter during his first years only to win them back later. Such would be his juggling act.[6]

When Epstein was called for a "trial weekend," he conducted services, gave sermons in Yiddish and English, and generally charmed his audience. When he attempted to walk through the community and sense the flavor of the area, he was interrupted by curious congregants interested in seeing and talking with the youthful scholar/cleric. He remained an additional day to speak before the Progressive Club, a social club of the East European Jews established in 1909 by those who had not felt comfortable or been welcomed into the German Jewish Standard Club. Many of the Progressive Club members had been associated with Congregation Beth Israel and were not affiliated with congregations. His speech, given in English, was very well received.

When Charles Glazer, acting for the congregation, wired a telegram offering the Ahavath Achim pulpit at a salary of $6,000 per year, Harry Epstein took time to consider the position. His father warned that the congregation included several individuals noted for their learning who might not accept him as their spiritual leader. The warning probably made Harry Epstein's decision easier. Here was to be another challenge besides an opportunity to go to a congregation where he was needed. He allowed the mustache begun in Oklahoma to grow to make himself look older.

He had become engaged to Reva (Rebecca) Chashesman, a very well educated young woman who was the daughter of Rabbi Judah Chashesman, the Orthodox leader of Chicago's Congregation Anshe Ticktin. They married in December 1928, a month after her graduation from the University of Chicago.

Rabbi Epstein had made inroads with the traditionalist elements even before his wedding in Chicago and his honeymoon in Florida and Cuba. As befitting a bachelor/rabbi, he lived with an older congregant's family. Congregational president Joseph Goldberg and his wife offered Epstein hospitality and assurance. He later eulogized Lena Goldberg as his "second mother."

As with many modern Orthodox rabbis, he had to prove his conpetence in the classical modes of rabbinic activity. He taught classes, or, more accurately, study sessions, in the Mishnah and the Talmud, meeting regularly with Rabbi Klinitsky, David Hadas (father of Rabbi Gershon Hadas and Columbia University classicist Moses Hadas), I. J. Paradies, David Gershon, and Charles Glazer, fine Hebraicists. Hadas was perhaps typical of these adult student/ scholars. He owned a used clothing store on Decatur Street, a major avenue of Atlanta's retail center disproportionately represented by Jewish merchants. During the day he was as likely to be pouring over Talmudic commentary as to be selling merchandise. When Epstein sought a source of an esoteric text, Hadas could usually provide it. And yet, Epstein more than held his own in these exchanges. His education and intellect served him well, and he gained the respect of these laymen, ultimately illustrated when they rose as he entered the room.[7]

The showcase of Epstein's talents for the general congregation and a pivotal step along the path to acceptance would be the High Holidays. Not only did all of the members attend, but so did local nonmembers and people from surrounding cities and towns. The holidays assumed a social as well as a religious significance. Here was an opportunity for people to visit the big city; to see and be seen by others and to refresh old acquaintanceships. These were also the holiest and most solemn days of the Jewish year. For the new rabbi, Rosh Hashanah and Yom Kippur took on the meaning of the colonial Puritan election sermon, a chance to prove himself, or to disappoint his audience. He would either establish a moral tone and interest and entertain his audience, or he would fail. By all accounts, Epstein succeeded. The services went smoothly. So necessary to attract the young adults and reassure the conservatives, he presented his sermons eloquently and with reasoned moderation. The innovative explanation of the background of specific prayers added to the significance of the renditions. Rabbi Epstein passed this test with high marks. People would return to hear and worship with him again, and congregational membership would likely grow.

Occasionally, Epstein adjusted his techniques to accommodate his different constituencies. He inaugurated an "early" eight o'clock Friday night service to attract the younger congregants into the shul while still allowing them time to attend the 9:30 showing at the local movie theater. On the first Sabbath eve that this service was attempted, he was locked out of the sanctuary by traditionalists who believed such services to be inappropriate. One of the young men climbed through a window, and the service proceeded. Yet, Epstein learned the need to explain to and confide in the older generation. He went to these people to ask if it was not better to conduct such services, and thus to keep their children practicing Jews, than to close one's eyes to changing circumstances and lose them altogether.

Henceforth, the rabbi spoke with the elders before initiating change, or he explained innovation after gradually acclimating them to it. The latter was the case with mixed seating. Women's seating went from a balcony to a separate section on the main floor. The ribbon dividing men from women grew smaller until some families broke the boundary and the line disappeared. How could men force older women to walk upstairs, the rabbi benevolently argued.

Similar arguments were used to introduce responsive and English readings, a new prayer book, and English sermons even on the High Holidays. (High Holiday sermons were also given in Yiddish until the congregation moved from its Washington Street location in 1958). The service became orderly and decorous and thus acceptable to a middle-class clientele, and nonetheless still traditional enough to ward off the loss of the old-timers. Harry Epstein, like Jung, Lookstein, and the other modern Orthodox adherents, illustrated a willingness to compromise on forms to maintain the essence of the religion.

The transmission of this religious essence was a fundamental objective of the new leader. To him, this transfer meant education of the broadest kind. The United Hebrew School, which Epstein now directed, switched to a well-organized, more-strenuous curriculum. Each year of study had defined subject matter and objectives. The Bible school was reorganized as a four-year graduated program leading to a confirmation ceremony. A high level of Hebrew proficiency was expected of bar mitzvah candidates. The bat mitzvah with individual ceremonies (as opposed to the more common but still innovative group ceremony on a specific day set aside each year) was also introduced. Incentives were provided for the Sunday Bible school students. Regular textbooks, report cards, and formal graduation ceremonies were added to the program. Participation grew to the point that classes had to be moved to the Crew Street School. A capable principal and qualified teachers were employed and encouraged to attend the new Institute of Jewish Studies. A regional young people's forum drew noted speakers to the biweekly winter gatherings.

Epstein instigated the establishment of a brotherhood, which supported the thirteen-person choir (described as a unique innovation in Orthodox congregations when it began under the training of a non-Jew, Emilio Volpi, in 1934). The brotherhood also sponsored services, held banquets to raise money for the congregation, maintained the bulletin (established by Epstein), and organized lecture series. The sisterhood, formed earlier by Rabbi Hirmes's wife, gained new meaning as Rabbi and Mrs. Epstein led Jewish book review meetings and conducted classes in basic Judaism, Jewish history, and holiday cooking and customs. Rabbi Epstein planned the first sisterhood Sabbath, and women were allowed for the first time on the bima (podium). When the congregation moved northward, the sisterhood assumed a major voice in the planning of the new edifice and raised the funds for the kitchen facilities and the lower parking lot. It was already sponsoring one of the first congregation-affiliated nursery schools, a junior congregation, and Brownie and Girl Scout troops. Numerous speakers made presentations to the congregation, and cultural programs were fostered.

The path to growth had been opened. Congregational membership and school attendance skyrocketed so that Ahavath Achim became the seventh- or eighth largest Orthodox congregation in the country. As the members moved north, some individuals formed a northside minyan, which became Congregation Adas Yeshurun (later renamed Beth Jacob) in 1936. Discussion ensued, resulting in the offshoot's reuniting with the parent body, which agreed to build a branch in the new neighborhood. An educational center also was established on Tenth Street.

The Depression slowed some of the activities and curtailed the bulletin and Institute of Jewish Studies altogether. The salaries of the teachers and the rabbi (who had voluntarily reduced his contractual income earlier) were not paid for months at a time. Teachers were housed in the homes of wealthier congregants, and the rabbi had to borrow to survive.

A congregation in New Orleans solicited Epstein's candidacy for its pulpit. He responded enthusiastically and actually accepted the appointment after spending a weekend in the city. However, although the position would have meant an increase in compensation and new challenges, he finally reconsidered and cast his lot permanently with Atlanta. Ahavath Achim's Board of Trustees granted him a tenured contract in 1938, only ten years after his installation.

Atlanta Jewry had not witnessed such dynamism or such a variety of programs since David Marx had come to The Temple three decades earlier. Certainly, the totality of these endeavors was unique for Atlanta's East European Jewish community. Nonetheless, from a different perspective, Epstein's Ahavath Achim traveled in the center of national trends. The national tendencies were stimulated by the thought of Mordecai Kaplan and others who were revitalizing American Jewry. These people experimented with model schools, emphasized the centrality of Jewish culture and life, and transformed the synagogue into the community center. In small cities with concentrated populations and limited resources, like Atlanta, the educational alliance/community center provided the athletic facilities. Individual congregations, exemplified by Ahavath Achim, offered a meaningful alternative to the limited synagogue as religious ceremonial headquarters model.[8]

National trends are again highlighted as Rabbi Epstein's career and programs are compared with those of two of his rabbinical colleagues in similar environs. Epstein had been asked to consider a position with Birmingham's three-year-old Congregation Beth-El in 1929. The synagogue wanted a rabbi who supported modern Orthodoxy, and there was a possibility of a joint appointment with neighboring Knesset Israel. Epstein refused, but he later recommended Rabbi Abraham J. Mesch, who ultimately filled the slot in 1935. During the intervening years Beth-El employed a rabbi who was forced to resign for health reasons, and another who pushed the congregation too far and too fast in the direction of modernity. Mesch, like Epstein, would proceed with greater deliberation. As Mesch's anniversaries arose through the years, Rabbi Epstein was called on to give the major speeches. The two also worked closely together at various Southeastern conferences.[9]

Mesch had been educated at the Hebrew Theological College and had spent a year at an Israeli yeshiva before receiving smicha from Rabbi Kook. Like Epstein, he earned a Ph.D. from the Illinois College of Law and a Th.D. from the Central School of Religion. At Beth-El, Mesch reinvigorated the Hebrew and Sunday school programs, gave new meaning to the services, and delivered sermons in

English. He, too, offered Yiddish sermons as well until the late 1940s. A junior congregation was created, and the sisterhood stressed Jewish learning and aid to the congregation. A choir was added for Friday night services, as was a biweekly forum to discuss topics of interest.

Mesch served as a chaplain during the Second World War at a local military installation, inspired Zionist activity as president of the local Zionist organizations, and involved himself with and led an interfaith ministerial association. All of these were activities mirroring Epstein's involvement in Atlanta. Mesch was deeply committed to the National Conference of Christians and Jews, as was Epstein. Beth-El grew until it became the largest congregation in Alabama and boasted of being one of the largest Orthodox centers in the South. The members grew more active in community affairs and, as they did, became more acceptable to and more accepting of the German Jews.

Mesch and Epstein helped form the Southeast section of the Union of Orthodox Congregations and participated actively in regional programs. Both men built educational centers and guided their congregations into expanded facilities. The Birmingham congregation affiliated with the United Synagogue of America in 1944, and Ahavath Achim followed at a slower pace, eight years later. With affiliation into the Conservative movement, Rabbis Mesch and Epstein assumed important and active positions in the Rabbinical Assembly's Southeast region. These two friends thus shared career experiences and a common vision of their congregations' futures.

They were joined in their endeavors by Rabbi Hirsch Heiman. Minneapolis, Minnesota's Congregation Knesseth Israel had gone from the old-time Orthodox shul established in 1888, one year after Ahavath Achim, to be the major sponsor of a chief rabbi for the entire city in 1902, to having the young members supporting the engagement of a rabbi who could conduct Friday night services and give sermons in English by 1914. When Rabbi Heiman was called to the pulpit in 1931, he had just completed his studies in Palestine. Born in Lithuania, Heiman was trained at the Slobodka yeshiva and traveled to Hebron as another one of the original students with Epstein. He received smicha from Moshe Mordecai Epstein, Epstein's brother-in-law, Meltzer (who had moved to the Etz Chaim yeshiva in Jerusalem), and Rabbi Kook. At Minneapolis, Heiman instigated the organization of a men's club to meet the needs of the younger members, created study groups for boys of different ages, and worked actively for the city federation, talmud torah, and Jewish Family Welfare and Children's Home. Typically, the men's club acted to perpetuate tradition by treating modern Jewish problems and by reaching out to the children of old-time members by making the synagogue a center of Jewish life. Heiman was a member of the Rabbinical Council of the Union of Orthodox Rabbis and served on the national boards of Mizrachi and the United Palestine Appeal. Rabbi Epstein accepted the latter's invitation to deliver the keynote address at the congregation's fiftieth anniversary.[10]

Jung and Lookstein, Mesch and Heiman, and Harry Epstein illustrate the evolution of the Orthodox camp during the 1920s, 1930s, and 1940s. They all contended with the problem of identity as they moved their congregations from generation to generation. They also exemplify the variations of change available as alternatives. Whereas Mesch's congregation became Conservative several years before Ahavath Achim, Heiman retained more tradition, and his congregation remains Orthodox even today. Mixed seating and bat mitzvah were too radical for the latter. From this perspective, modern Orthodoxy did not lead inevitably to Conservative affiliation, and individuals did have significant choices to make. Why did an Epstein go further than a Heiman, or even a Lookstein or a Jung? The answer to this most-difficult question can remain only conjecture. Perhaps there was something in Epstein's personality more accepting of what, at the time, seemed like inevitable change. Perhaps in Atlanta he saw a vibrant, influential Reform congregation and a seemingly backward Orthodox shul struggling to stay afloat. Perhaps there was a reaction to his father and his uncle, or something in his eclectic education. Perhaps elements within Ahavath Achim pushed Rabbi Epstein further than he might have wanted to proceed. In any case, the young rabbi, with many of his contemporaries who represented varieties of adjustment, realized that modern Orthodoxy provided a way for the immigrants and their children to come together.[11]

Americanized, European-born rabbis trained in the Slobodka method, although able to lead in several directions, possessed the structural tools, intellectual prowess, and personalities to fathom the problems of the 1920s and 1930s and to mold the old and the new together. Not only did they interact with their myriad congregational audiences, they also consciously or unconsciously recreated the previous German-American rabbinic role of ethnic brokers, or intermediaries to the non-Jewish community. In fact, service and interaction in secular society reinforced their positions within their upwardly mobile congregations much as it had earlier for the German Jewish rabbis. They performed these functions while leading their followers into Jewish and nonsectarian community service and activism on behalf of the establishment of a state of Israel.

How can Harry Epstein's personal contributions be assessed? Whereas he may have pioneered especially in the South such innovations as choirs—and gentile trained at that—and individual bat mitzvah Sabbath ceremonies, his real significance is that he became a regional spokesman and role model for others to emulate. He articulated his mission clearly and became a conduit for change.

His positions as spokesman, role model, and guide can be illustrated through several avenues of inquiry. First, Epstein's sermons included frequent and lengthy expositions of Orthodoxy's strengths. In these sermons he emphasized that Orthodoxy was superior in that it adjusted external practices "in accordance with the times," while simultaneously encouragng observance, knowledge, and commitment. Orthodoxy thus maintained faith and tradition through a modern medium and effectively opposed assimilation.

That his congregants recognized his message and supported the mission is shown through their explanations of their clubs and activities. He had made Ahavath Achim into "a mighty force in the preservation of American Israel," they wrote. The religious school dealt primarily with the Bible to instill "a basic concept of Judaism." One of the congregation's critical sources of strength was "its unreserved dedication to and intelligent grasp of the totality of Judaism." These were phrases with special meanings that Epstein could have written himself. The community, too, accepted him as unique and still part of a pattern. In 1936 a *Southern Israelite* writer authored an article entitled "Modernizing Traditional Judaism." After describing Epstein's antecedents and education, Orin Borsten listed the various changes in Ahavath Achim observance under the rabbi.

Rabbi Epstein was defined as an exemplar of his type and as one who served as a role model for others throughout the United States espousing modern Orthodoxy. When congregations solicited his application to fill ministerial vacancies, they described themselves as modern Orthodox congregations and viewed him as a desirable candidate. Those who commended him for such positions—especially teachers from the Hebrew Theological College—also described him as a leading modern Orthodox practitioner. Finally, when Epstein delivered speeches throughout the Southeast, he was virtually always referred to in the newspaper accounts and advertisements as the region's leader in the new wave. That he gave so many speeches (including many for the installations of other rabbis and the dedications of their synagogues) reflected tremendous demand for his abilities, but especially for the exposition of his point of view. Epstein was part of a major transition in American Jewry even as he helped lead.[12]

5

Reaching Out to Different Communities

Rabbi Harry Epstein established a stable base of support within his congregation rather quickly as accentuated by his receipt of a life appointment after only a decade in Atlanta. He perceived his role and that of the congregation on a broad scale. His image fit perfectly with the needs and expectations of his congregants although these needs and expectations were not necessarily perceived at the time.

Many individuals in the congregation already had become active in Jewish communal affairs and had served as spokespeople of Atlanta's East European Jews to the German Jews. In his sermons Epstein encouraged them to expand their service as part of their Jewish social commitment. By the 1940s and 1950s, Ahavath Achim members had overtaken the former leadership in Jewish service agencies, again reflecting a trend visible in Jewish communities throughout America.[1]

Like his father, Harry Epstein taught by example. No other Orthodox rabbi in Atlanta, and few in the South, became as deeply involved with communal affairs beyond parochial issues like the supervision of kosher butchers and the building of a *mikveh* (ritual bath).[2] Epstein participated in the Jewish War Veterans and served as the honorary chaplain of local post 112. On the request of the warden, he served as Jewish chaplain at the Atlanta Penitentiary. During World War II he became a part-time chaplain at the local military installations. For many years he participated on the boards of trustees of the Atlanta Jewish Community Council, the Hebrew Orphans' Home, and the Bureau of Jewish Education.

Clearly, one of his most important contributions was given to the Atlanta Federation of Jewish Charities. The major social service agencies of both the East European and German Jewish communities had been federated between 1909 and 1912. Nonetheless, during and after the First World War a myriad of fund-raising groups, which reflected national divisions, were formed to meet the requirements of overseas relief. The need in Atlanta as elsewhere was to rationalize the fund-raising process to avoid conflict and waste. In Atlanta a critical meeting took place in which much of the city's Jewish leadership participated. The result was the creation of a Jewish Welfare Fund. This citywide effort remained vital until it was incorporated in 1967 into the present Atlanta Jewish Federation. Besides professionalizing fund raising, the new fund brought together the various Jewish subcommunities on a more equitable basis and thus helped lower barriers. Unlike previous efforts, the East Europeans could finally provide financial support commensurate with their desire for power. This participation bred respect and even business interaction on a different plane than the former intellectual associations between individuals. Rabbi Epstein played a major role in the 1936 meeting and served on the board of the new fund from its inception. He gave a critical speech dramatizing the plight of world Jewry, the need to subsidize medical and relief efforts within America, and the need to support educational endeavors, European and Palestinian yeshivas, Yeshiva College, and the Hebrew Theological College. Ahavath Achim's United Hebrew School, open to all children in the community, also received early funding.[3]

In 1950 Epstein served as the cochairperson of the Jewish Welfare Fund campaign with Rabbi Jacob Rothschild of The Temple. This collaboration was the first time in the city's history that two rabbis from the two major subcommunities worked together at such a high level. It symbolized to some extent the acceptance of the East European Jews by the German Jews and the coming of age of the East European community. It also represented a new high in rabbinical leadership. Rothschild and Epstein traveled to Europe and Israel together and met with national and international agency leaders, including those of the Joint Distribution Committee, the major conduit for allocating resources overseas.

This "Unity Campaign of 1950" was highly successful in raising funds for Holocaust relief and resettlement of immigrants into Israeli society. The two rabbis remained friendly acquaintances, occasionally playing high-scoring golf rounds together. They had previously been elected separately to the presidency of Gate City Lodge of B'nai B'rith. The world of the Orthodox rabbi and his congregation was expanding.

Rabbi Epstein admonished his congregants regularly about giving to federation campaigns. He took his message to other Southern cities also as he frequently launched their campaign drives. All was not totally rosy, however. Epstein might have become even more active in the federation had it not been for his relationship with the executive director. Edward Kahn had been hired to head the federation in 1928. A professional social worker, Kahn was a man of uncommon ability and drive, but one who wanted control and had no desire to share power with the local clergy. In this conflict of two strong individuals, the community probably came out the loser. The lack of regular interaction and cooperation continued as a pattern when Kahn was replaced with Max "Mike" Gettinger in 1964.

Beyond the confines of Atlanta, Harry Epstein became a state, regional, and national leader of Jewish organizations and thus encouraged participation of his congregants on those levels as well. Epstein was quickly singled out as a favored speaker throughout Georgia and the surrounding states for installations, anniversaries, building dedications, B'nai B'rith and similar organizational meetings, and fund-raising campaigns. From 1928 through the early 1950s the rabbi accepted numerous opportunities of this type. He even was asked to serve Jewish agencies in the hinterland. In 1937, for example, he spoke before the Hebrew Commercial Alliance of Fitzgerald, Georgia, and was made a member of its advisory board. He became a member of the commission on religious and educational participation for the American Jewish Tercenary Committee. He was on the arrangements committee of the Southeast regional Anti-Defamation League meeting for 1939 and received that organization's Abe Goldstein Human Relations Award in 1970. The rabbi was one of ten founding members of the Rabbinical Cabinet of the Jewish Theological Seminary. He spoke at the seminary when his brother Emanuel was presented a certificate of merit in 1975. Epstein served on the executive committee of the Union of Orthodox Congregations of America and on the Rabbinical Council. He became equally active in Conservative ranks after the congregation's change of affiliation. He gave numerous presentations and keynote speeches before the Southeast and Seaboard regions of the United Synagogue of America and won election to the presidency of the Southeast region Rabbinic Assembly in 1964. Nationally, his leadership positions included membership on the executive council of the Rabbinic Assembly and on its pivotal Commission on Jewish Law and Standards. He was opening the doors for and reinforcing important involvement of his congregants in Jewish communal affairs.[4]

Undoubtedly, Harry Epstein's greatest commitment and service on all levels were reserved for aid to European and Holy Land Jewry ultimately linked with Zionism. His interest in these intertwined areas obviously originates in his background. He followed his family's footsteps and his own experiences. Just as his uncle was cognizant of the need to remove his yeshiva from Lithuanian prejudice and persecution, so, too, Harry Epstein realized the continuing hardships faced by European Jewry during the 1920s. The younger Epstein's solution echoed that of the older man; the only way to ensure Jewish survival and a secure refuge for worldwide Jewry was through the establishment of a Jewish state in Israel.

Although providing a refuge was one key to Harry Epstein's desire for the creation of the state of Israel, it was not his only rationale. In fact, his perceptions of Zionism actually underwent transformation as circumstances changed. During the interwar period, a sense of *galut* stood almost equal in importance with a need for haven. The term *galut* meant exile and referred to the expulsion of the Jews from the ancient kingdom of Israel after the destruction of the second temple in Jerusalem. Jews consequently traveled from country to country seeking freedom, finding temporary respite, but finally becoming victims of persecution. They spread to the corners of the globe. The dispersal and settlement outside of Israel is called the diaspora. To a European Jewry that had experienced centuries of persecution, and to Rabbi Epstein, *galut* had thus assumed additional meaning. Epstein equated Zionism with the "effort of the Jewish people to fulfill its way of life, its nationhood." According to the rabbi, before Napoleon granted them rights and freedoms, Jews thought of themselves as a nation in exile besides being a religious group. The ultimate hope for European Jewry was a return to Israel. As they gained citizenship in the countries of Western Europe during the mid nineteenth century, they were allowed and encouraged to assimilate. Actually, the granting of rights was premised on a desire for their final absorption. The adjustment to freedom Epstein associated with the rise of Reform Judaism and its universalism. The Orthodox viewed freedom outside Israel as a transient situation, and the denaturing of the faith as anathema. As Epstein explained it, "To a very real extent, Zionism [is] synonymous with Judaism in the sense that return and only that to the land can make Judaism survive, flourish and continue its creative ability." In essence, being a complete Jew was impossible while in *galut*. He expected that the establishment of a Jewish state would then bring with it a renaissance of Jewish culture. Zionism was also part of the messianic promise "to alleviate Jewish misery" and bring an end to "humiliation [and] homelessness." It would nurture Jewish unity as well.[5]

As would be expected, Rabbi Epstein welcomed the establishment in 1948 of the State of Israel, and the refuge it provided for persecuted Jews. Yet, statehood brought changes in his stance on the concept and mission of Zionism. As Melvin Urofsky has described the dilemma facing so many American Zionists, "The state had been created; now what did one do?" To Harry Epstein, as to so many others, the Zionist dream was complete with the act of creation, and he felt little need to live in the country permanently as a personal act of fulfillment.

Epstein showed pride and support for Israel during the war for independence and the early years in which absorption of immigrants drained resources. This support was marshaled through the federation campaigns, especially as represented by his cochairmanship of the 1950 unity drive. Raising funds seemed to satisfy the commitment of American Jews of the era. But, as the secular state governed the new country, Epstein's image of Zionism as the center of Jewish life lost some of its luster. The actual state simply could not meet the spiritual and cultural needs of American Jewry as it grappled with very real worldly demands, nor did it appear to share these requirements. Religious observance and cooperation with diaspora Jews who refused to reside in Israel were not high on the agenda of Israeli leaders.[6]

In the troubled year of 1957, while Americans engaged in conflict over ending segregation in the public schools, Epstein warned Israel to integrate its people and overcome racial prejudice. In Israel's bar mitzvah year, 1960, the rabbi sermonized, "Survival in the presence of a Jewish state is something radically different from mere galut existence. We can no longer talk of 'Jewish contributions to civilization' as a reason for survival. It never was a good (convincing) argument . . . Jewish contributions will be made in Israel, labelled as Jewish, not anonymously, and much more effectively."

Nonetheless, while Jews in Israel helped those in the diaspora, Jews in the diaspora also had to continue to help those in Israel. Besides financial aid, "By studying and learning we can help Israel produce more poetry and literature. We can exchange scholars and students [to] help Torah to come out of Zion." *Galut* had changed from expecting a Jewish revival emanating from a messianically endowed homeland, to having to provide a nurturing environment in promotion of the culture of Israel.

With the 1967 Six Day War, Epstein's image of Zionism and the relationship between American and Israeli Jews again underwent metamorphosis. Now, the Israeli Jews were fighting for a mission and a right, he surmised, and the job of the Zionist, once more, became treating the needs of survival and overcoming hardship. Israel's allies had been slow in coming to its relief and quick to condemn. Epstein concluded that "only Jews care about Israel." After a visit to Israel and Europe in 1969, the rabbi reported that he was overwhelmed with Israel and its accomplishments. He predicted that "victory will come" over hardship and danger because of Israel's most significance resource: the "passionate determination" of its people. If Israel failed, however, it would mean the destruction of all Jewry. A trip the following year brought a call before a United Jewish Appeal conference for American Jewish solidarity and the increase in contributions in time of need.

After the Yom Kippur War of 1973, Rabbi Epstein's cause became more political again, but now also defensive. He felt called on to repeat the arguments for Israel's right to exist. He denounced Yasir Arafat's 1974 welcome from the United Nations and the equation of Zionism with racism. Denunciations of Ambassador Andrew Young's performance as a diplomat were followed by defense of Israel's claim to Judea and Samaria and the 1982 "Peace for Galilee" campaign in Lebanon. But people were despairing in the 1970s. Epstein counseled that they should expect ideals to be achievable, and that they should look forward to the good results of Zionism. As the Epsteins led an Ahavath Achim mission to the Holy Land, he told his receptive audience that everything was possible.[7]

Epstein's evolving views vis-à-vis Zionism were somewhat of an amalgam and, in that way, were probably more typical than original. Individuals have interpreted Zionism and come to the movement from many different vantage points. This disparity has contributed to what Urofsky has called "the infinite variety of the Zionist movement." Leo Pinsker and the founders of the Hovevei Zion (Lovers of Zion) society, responding to the Russian pogroms of 1880, advocated colonization of Palestine as a practical prelude to the (unlikely) creation of a future state and emphasized the Jewish heritage. Theodor Herzl saw the Jewish people as an anomaly, a people without a nation, and he concluded that only with statehood could they survive and contribute to civilization. A new nation would alleviate prejudice and end the years of suffering. Jewish socialists like Ber Borochov and Nachman Syrkin posited a Jewish state as a means to "spiritual redemption" in a classless society. Ahad Ha'am (Asher Ginsberg) pictured a Zion that would serve as a center of Jewish culture and spirit. The poet indicated that the homeland would be unimportant without cultural redemption and that actual residence in a political state was not necessary for participation in the mission. Isaac Jacob Reines and other religious Zionists who supported Mizrachi associated a homeland as a religious mecca and assumed that ritual observance was essential for any legitimate Zionist state.[8]

American Zionists differed from their European counterparts largely because they did not experience the virtually constant anti-Semitism and tenuousness of Jewish life in the old world. Here, citizenship, rising status, and basic acceptance were the norms. Thus, American Jews tended to see a Jewish state as a refuge for European Jews but not as a potential home for American Jews, who gradually transformed the concept of *galut* into an acceptable American Jewish cultural revival in the diaspora. To Henrietta Szold, future founder of Hadassah, and Harry Friedenwald, supporters of Hoveve Zion during the early twentieth century, participation in the Zionist movement would discourage assimilation as it fostered Jewish dignity and a cultural revival. Louis Brandeis, Supreme Court justice and pivotal figure in American Zionist ranks for decades, integrated Zionism with American Progressivism. For Brandeis and his supporters, the prophetic values of Judaism and the American liberal tradition were interchangeable. Many American Zionists came to the movement through what Allon Gal defines as "the mission motif." From this extension of Brandeis's conception, a Jewish state would contribute to a revival of the religion's social justice message and provide a light to lead the world on the path toward ethical and harmonious coexistence. Arnold Eisen, contemplating the changing perceptions of *galut,* argues that American Zionists separated the end of exile into physical and metaphysical dimensions. A state was essential as a refuge for European Jewry, whereas Americans could achieve a redemptive state of fulfillment without moving to Israel. For Solomon Schechter, head of the Jewish Theological Seminary and formulator of Conservative Judaism, Mordecai Kaplan, seminary faculty member and creator of the Reconstructionist approach, and Abraham Joshua Heschel, a leading Jewish ethicist of the mid twentieth century, morality, spirituality, and peoplehood could be translated into a state of mind and heart approachable anywhere that Jews could live freely and practice their religious observance. Adherence to Zionism furthered the rejuvenation process.

In his early years, then, Harry Epstein's ideas were a reflection of his European and first-generation outlook. As he and his congregants enjoyed the benefits of upward mobility and traveled further along the road of acculturation, the changing conceptualization of Zionism reflected the American realities and hopes for American Jewry besides the needs of brethren elsewhere and ultimate pride in their accomplishments. Rabbi Epstein's actions paralleled his thoughts.

The first recorded Zionist activity in which Epstein participated in Atlanta was a Zionist organization district meeting in December 1928. Rabbi Geffen offered greetings at this Palestine Evening Program, and Epstein gave a speech on Zionism. The following April, Epstein participated in the first annual conference on Palestine of the Southern region of the United Palestine Appeal. He was very moved by the guest of honor, Dr. Nahum Sokolow, whom he called "the dean of Zionism."[9]

A horrible tragedy seemed to energize Rabbi Epstein four months later. Arab mobs unleashed a reign of terror in Palestine. The Hebron yeshiva was a key mob objective. As noted earlier, many students, including his younger brother, lost their lives. Harry Epstein assumed the chairmanship of the Georgia Palestine Emergency Campaign and went to the airwaves. He delivered a radio address entitled "Palestine Memorial Hour," in which he denounced Arab barbarism and emphasized the desire of Jews to work with the Arabs in the rebuilding of Palestine—concepts espoused by mainstream Zionists. In a series of speeches before civic and church groups, Jews and gentiles, the rabbi outlined Jewish claims to the Holy Land and provided evidence of the recognition of those claims.

Through the 1930s and into the 1940s, Epstein continued to speak out on WGST radio and wherever speaking engagements took him. He spoke in Chicago on the twenty-seventh anniversary of Theodore Herzl's death before the Keren Kayemeth League (the Jewish National Fund, or J.N.F., formed in 1901). His words launched

Atlanta's J.N.F. campaign. He addressed Zionist district rallies and the first annual joint Hadassah/Zionist district meeting (1938). As a protégé of Gedaliah Bublick, editor of the *Judisches Tageblatt,* a noted Orthodox Yiddish newspaper, Epstein was appointed secretary of a Mizrachi convention. He spoke to the National Council of Jewish Women, a largely upper-class, German Jewish organization; to annual Southeast regional conventions of the Zionist Organization of America; to leadership retreats of the Zionist Youth Commissions; and to Hadassah meetings throughout Georgia and the South. He stressed the purchase and reclamation of the land, successes thus far, and peaceful coexistence.[10]

In 1937, Lord Peel submitted a Royal Commission report to the British Parliament advocating the partition of Palestine into Jewish and Arab sections. Epstein, like David Ben-Gurion and other Zionists, interpreted this altered British policy as a withdrawal from the original promise of the Balfour Declaration. As part of the Zionist movement, Epstein denounced Britain's perfidy, but he later accepted partition as a condition for statehood.

He found quislings closer to home. American Reform Jews had rejected Jewish nationhood since the Pittsburgh Platform of 1885. With a few notable exceptions, anti-or non-Zionist opinion held sway until the 1930s. The platform adopted in 1938 in Columbus finally aligned the Reform movement on the side of a Jewish state. Yet, Judge Jerome Frank, of the isolationist America First Committee and the American Council for Judaism, continued to denounce Zionism into the 1940s. Epstein took issue with Frank's statements as he preached the pluralism of Louis D. Brandeis.

What made Epstein's pleas so poignant and immediate was his early recognition of the imminent destruction of European Jewry. As early as 1934 he emphasized the dangers posed by Nazism to European Jewish survival. Next, he denounced the Nuremburg Decrees, which abrogated Jewish citizenship and rights, and then the government-promoted riots known as *kristallnacht,* the night of the shattered glass. Epstein raised money to save as many German and Polish Jews as possible. During 1939 he continually beseeched his congregants to contribute funds. A typical sermon was "The Tragic Fate of 8,000,000 Jews Today." By 1940 he used the term *genocide,* and, during the early 1940s, he described death by hunger and disease, the rise and destruction of the ghettoes, and the existence and purpose of the concentration camps. Epstein participated in nationally called services to commemorate the Warsaw ghetto uprising and other such acts of resistance. Like other rabbis, Epstein denounced the British "White Paper" of 1939, which drastically limited Jewish immigration into Palestine. In 1942 he informed his congregation that the State Department was aware of Hitler's plan to exterminate European Jewry and had decided not to publicize the Final Solution. At the same time that Stephen S. Wise, a national spokesman with the ear of President Franklin Roosevelt, pursued a policy of quiet persuasion that practically acquiesced to the State Department position, Epstein joined the more activist Abba Hillel Silver in advocating open public pressure to push Roosevelt to action.[11]

A series of crises confronted American and world Jewry during the 1930s and 1940s. Such leaders as Nahum Goldmann, Silver and Wise, Chaim Weizmann, and Emanuel Neumann jockeyed for positions of power and prestige, debated competing policies and practices, and created numerous agencies. The meetings were legion because the stakes were so high. Every action of Hitler and every European development required response, and involved debate. How best could Jews respond to changes in British policy toward a potential Jewish state and immigration to Palestine? How should they respond to the inaction of the American government? Should Jews raise money, or lobby members of Congress, demonstrate, or practice private diplomacy? Should the emphasis be on the immediate establishment of a Jewish state, and what should be the size and nature of that state? How would American Jewish reactions impact on the position of Jews within American society? Should and would power shift from European to American Jewry? Whichever decisions were made, the individual and the group in the minority would be disgruntled. People went their own way, but the Holocaust would not be prevented.

Little or no indication of the national and international rivalries within Zionist ranks surfaces in the Epstein correspondence or sermons. This omission becomes even more surprising when it is recognized that fissures existed also within the South between Zionists, non-Zionists, and anti-Zionists. Yet, there was greater homogeneity over a representative congress scheme, promoted nationally by Gedaliah Bublick among others, which would detract from the conservative power of the upper-class German Jews. Greater cooperation seemed to be the rule also concerning fund raising for overseas relief. Issues of mismanagement of funds, and divisions between Weizmann supporters who advocated cultural enrichment alongside practical nation building, and the Brandeisian support for efficiency and single-minded preparation of Palestine did not appear to phase Zionists as much on the grass-roots scene. Whether Orthodox traditional or even Reform, Atlanta Jewry exhibited more concern for doing what was necessary for Jewish survival and the regeneration of religious culture and spirit through adherents to Jewish nationalism than bickering over means. The central thread running through Epstein's thoughts and actions was the desire to do whatever was called for. Thus, he would raise money, speak, organize, interact with the community, work in behalf of practical, cultural or religious agencies, travel, and lobby. Although he probably had favorite national leaders and disliked others, any action contributing to a refuge for the persecuted in Europe and promoting Judaism garnered Epstein's support.

Harry Epstein became a minor player on the national scene, and a key player regionally, as he was called on to articulate and execute national policies locally. In February 1936 he traveled to Washington as a Zionist district delegate to a national conference on Palestine. More than one thousand two hundred representatives attended the gathering, which was the culmination of a meeting that had taken place the previous year in Switzerland. Epstein termed the Washington meeting "a milestone" because it brought together Zionists and non-Zionists, as they jointly responded to the tragedy taking place in Germany, and in favor of the long-term hope of Israel. Epstein witnessed no debate or division. Individuals had come to hear the presentations of leaders and to approve previously agreed upon resolutions. It was decided to raise an additional million dollars for the United Palestine Appeal and ten million dollars to save German Jews. Palestine, it was stated, now played the very pivotal and practical role of safety valve for German and Polish Jewry.[12]

Epstein became a member of the National Council for Palestine and went on the road. He helped organize the five-state Southeast Zionist regional convention in 1938, and he wrote "Zionists meet in Historic Hour" for the second annual meeting, which he helped host in Atlanta. In 1940 he gave the keynote presentation launching the August United Jewish Appeal for refugee relief and received a letter of appreciation from national chairman Jonah B. Wise. Stephen S. Wise had sent Epstein a telegram requesting his aid in launching the Miami campaign since Epstein was "the strongest representative of our cause" in the South. Epstein agreed to the call for aid and also agreed to preside over the Atlanta district Mizrachi the year the war formally began in Europe. In 1943 and in 1946 he was elected state chairman of the Zionist Organization of America's Jewish National Fund. In 1944 the regional president announced the "Georgia Nachal," the purchase of one thousand dunums of land in Palestine for $25,000. Epstein planned, organized, and led the drive to successful completion.

During and shortly after World War II a series of national conferences took place with Epstein's participation. The conventions followed in the spirit of that of 1936, with perhaps even greater urgency. The National Council for Palestine of the United Palestine Appeal met in June 1942. Delegate Epstein was one of only four men to present resolutions at this New York gathering. The American Jewish Conference, a five-day meeting held in 1943, cited the four million already murdered by the Nazis. A series of resolutions was approved denouncing the genocide and in support of a Jewish state. Other resolutions advocated the strengthening of Youth Aliyah and denigrated the anti-Zionist American Council for Judaism. Epstein had been chosen over two other candidates in a citywide Atlanta election. One of his columns outlining the responsibilities of the conference was published in the bulletin of a San Francisco congregation.

The end of the war brought little respite. Now, the needs of those in displaced persons camps, of those attempting to break the British blockade of Palestine, and of those creating the Jewish state were priorities. Epstein served as a delegate to both the World Zionist Convention and the American Jewish Conference meetings in 1946. The ensuing year a community thanksgiving sponsored by the Atlanta Zionist Council in honor of a Jewish state was held at Ahavath Achim with Rabbis Geffen and Cohen, the latter of Sephardic Congregation Or VeShalom, speaking.

In January 1948, Epstein received an urgent telegram from New York concerning the rise of Arab warfare in rejection of statehood. He urged his congregants to wire President Harry Truman and Georgia Senators Walter F. George and Richard B. Russell to support the supply of military equipment and to establish a multinational force to enable the Yishuv, the Palestine Jewish community, to carry out the United Nations mandate for independence.

As previously indicated, Epstein served as cochairman of the Atlanta Jewish Welfare Fund's 1950 campaign, which was geared toward the needs of the dispossessed, particularly through immigration to Israel. The federation assumed the responsibilities of the old organizations as time went on, but, by 1957, Epstein took the initiative in trying to rejuvenate the Atlanta commitment to the Jewish National Fund. He received a letter of encouragement from the national executive secretary as he sponsored a J.N.F. dinner. The Council of Rabbis of the Israel Bond organization included Epstein among its members, and he was awarded the State of Israel Freedom Award in 1971. He was a member of the executive committee of the Joint Distribution Committee at the time of his retirement, and he and Reva were honored at an Israeli Bond Dinner in 1985. They were given Israel's Heritage Award the following year.

Still, his greatest efforts after 1959 seem to have been devoted to the Organization for Rehabilitation through Training (O.R.T.). This agency emphasized the provision of vocational and technical education so that Jews in Israel and other countries outside the United States would not be dependent on charity. Their lives would thus gain dignity, meaning, and freedom. Epstein was founder and honorary chairman of Atlanta Men's O.R.T. When he was given the O.R.T. Man of the Year Award in 1971, he was cited by the national chairman for mobilizing the city, state, and region so quickly and for making Atlanta the largest center of O.R.T. members in the South. Besides his typical speaking engagements, he attended national and world conferences (in Geneva in 1970 and Jerusalem in 1974), and he served on American O.R.T. Federation's national board as well as on its executive committee. From 1964 he spoke about American responsibility toward Russian Jews in the same fashion that he had for other oppressed Jews previously. Harry Epstein successfully sponsored a resolution sent to the State Department to pressure the Soviet Union to allow immigration at the 1971 national conference.

Much has been written recently concerning American Jewish involvement—or, more pointedly, lack of effective influence—in the saving of European Jewry. With Harry Epstein, we have a case study of a rabbi removed from the seats of power in New York and Washington and with little political clout who nonetheless did everything he could to bring the issues forward and provide assistance. Within a year of Hitler's rise, Epstein was aware of the very real threat Nazism posed to the Jews of Europe, and he brought the problem to the public's attention. He, along with a few other individuals, including Sol Benamy, Julian Boehm, and Robert Travis, revitalized Zionism in Atlanta. Atlanta served as a hub of the Southeast, with Epstein as a critical spoke. Money was raised to help those who remained in Europe, to facilitate immigration, and to build a homeland to house the refugees from persecution. Epstein participated in national conferences that attempted to unify American Jewish responses, multiply the giving of donations, and influence public policy. He adjusted his thoughts and actions to changing conditions. Although he was not satisfied, and although he believed that American Jewry was too unorganized and unprepared to provide sufficient assistance, Harry Epstein deserves credit as a local and regional leader acting under extremely difficult circumstances.

Epstein's efforts in behalf of European Jewry and Zionism nurtured interaction between different communities. His efforts gained the respect of German and Sephardic Jews in Atlanta and forged bonds with Jewish communities in Georgia and throughout the Southeast. He also developed contacts and recognition on the national and international levels. As he did so, he fostered his congregation's relationship with these same communities. Epstein's actions thus tended to break down barriers and build bridges.[14]

The same can be said of his association with the Christian community of Atlanta. Once again, Rabbi Epstein was a path breaker. Previously, David Marx, spiritual leader of the German Reform congregation, had been the spokesman of the Jews to the gentiles. The East European rabbis typically were more fluent in Yiddish than English, and they narrowly confined their interests to congregation and intra-religious affairs. Epstein's actions thus eased the way for the relative acceptance of East European Jews in Atlanta, a concomitant of the group's socioeconomic advances.

Just twelve weeks after his arrival in Atlanta, Epstein had been asked to speak on the radio. He recalls having numerous questions put to him from the non-Jewish audiences concerning ritual, beliefs, and the Bible. His listeners viewed him as a voice of authority from "the Chosen People," so to speak, and they were amazed at many of his revelations concerning the nature of Judaism. During the years, Epstein had many opportunities to teach in this fashion. He tended to emphasize brotherhood, but he did not shy away from explaining overseas problems, including anti-Semitism. In 1929 a *Southern Israelite* editorial advocated the greater use of radio for "encouraging a more perfect understanding between Jew and Gentile," and it praised Epstein's frequent appearances on WSB radio as a model.[15]

In other efforts at outreach, the rabbi spoke at dedications throughout the state and at interfaith forums and services. The *Atlanta Constitution* sought him out for a contribution as a spokesman for the Jewish community when they wanted to abstract sermons of local clergy. He was especially active in behalf of the National Conference of Christians and Jews and received that organization's award for "contributions to improve human relations." He spoke at the memorial service for the Veterans of Foreign Wars and on Confederate Memorial Day and offered prayers to open both the Georgia and national House of Representatives. He received several "Beaver Awards" from WSB radio for being the busiest newsmaker of the week.

Ever the activist, early in his career Epstein became very involved with the Atlanta Community Chest. His commitment heightened with the Depression. He became chairman of the Emergency Relief Committee in 1931. He beseeched the public "to fight hunger and want" with double giving to charity as the debt "the fortunate has owed the unfortunate." It probably did not go unnoticed that he couched his request with reference to *tzedekah*—the Jewish concept of righteous giving. People should not give out of pity, but for the sake of justice. Relief was not alms, but rather the symbol of an obligation people had toward each other.[16]

Although outwardly against mixing religion and politics, Rabbi Epstein did not remain silent when a principle was at stake—even if his opinion clashed with community mores. In 1938 he asked his fellow Atlantans to vote for a six-and-one-half-million-dollar bond issue for the city and county to stimulate business, make needed improvements, and overcome unemployment. The bond issue would make the area eligible for New Deal dollars. He counseled that, whether or not his Southern listeners agreed with national policy, needed programs were available, and the region should take advantage of the opportunity. As a civic booster with a difference, the rabbi noted that "The way to democracy lies in increased happiness—physical and moral—of its citizenry. The way to happiness lies in the direction of health, education, and in the general program of social service. . . . We . . . are looking out today upon a frantic, desperate, panic stricken world. We are seeing a world gone mad." As Americans, we should choose "schools rather than guns."[17]

Nine years later in a WGST-CBS broadcast of "Church of the Air," Epstein selected as his topic "Atomic Morality." Again, the world was in chaos. This time he advocated a revival of morality based on "tried and tested Biblical ideas" through a "world government." He viewed the Democratic battle for control of the eighty-first Congress in 1948 as a fight between David and Goliath. The previous Congress had "betrayed people" with the termination of price controls, cuts in housing, farm subsidies and social security, and passage of the Taft-Hartley Act. Epstein clearly declared support for President Truman and the liberal agenda. He just as forcefully denigrated the McCarthyites, whom Epstein believed were "harming the entire basis upon which democracy rests." The rabbi supported a code of ethics for congressional committees.

In 1968 he voiced ambiguous support for the Vietnam conflict. He was frustrated with being manipulated, but he viewed intervention as necessary to halt communism, which destroyed human dignity. Yet "nothing in life is all black or all white." he continued. "Life consists mostly of gray areas." He pointed to the Jewish acceptance of different types of war and allowances for conscientious objection based on one's personal beliefs. He praised the Supreme Court's ruling broadly defining the grounds for conscientious objector status. He did not resort to polemics when referring to Watergate and Richard Nixon. Nixon was a president of spectacular achievements with regard to peace. But, the rabbi continued, an individual is "a sum total of minor acts day by day that add up to give a picture of what a person is like." Greatness in one area neither overcame, nor mitigated, extreme failings in another.

On a different subject, Epstein declared that Judaism advocated woman's rights. It always "sought by law to dignify and sanctify the status of every human being. . . ." Women had the same obligations as men except that they were free of some burdens because of their domestic responsibilities. Women could own property and engage in business. Single women were equal to men in every way. Woman's liberation was more than equal pay for equal work. It included the granting and allowance of equal status, equal respect, and equal rights. It was in this regard that the rabbi advocated bat mitzvah, mixed seating, and participation in services. Still a traditionalist to some extent, however, he blanched at the idea of women reading from the Torah. This innovation, which his successor adopted, went too far for Epstein.

Finally, the rabbi did not mince words when it came to anti-Semitism. He denounced the Vatican II Council's rejection of anti-Semitism as too little and too late, and as but "a nice gesture." Epstein opined, "When prejudice has been instilled for all these generations a resolution cannot undo what has been planted in the hearts for centuries." Actions would have to follow words. To a mixed-audience National Conference of Christians and Jews colloquy on Christianity and anti-Semitism, he declared, "Anti-Semitism has its roots in Christianity."

The litmus test for anyone's social responsibility in the South lies in the area of social justice for blacks. It is widely conceded that, while a few Southern rabbis were courageous enough to speak out, most either accepted Southern mores, or more frequently remained silent to protect the vulnerable positions of their congregations. Although Rabbi Epstein regrets that he did not take a strong, activist role in favor of the civil rights movement, his papers disclose a record of relatively outspoken support even on many of the most-controversial issues. In 1948 he spoke to black and white high school students on brotherhood in a program sponsored by the National Council of Christians and Jews. To the separate, segregated audiences he emphasized the need for unity and understanding to overcome prejudices in a difficult world. During the same year, Epstein supported the courageous stand of the Democratic Party in behalf of civil rights at its nominating convention and in its platform. As other Southerners hailed Strom Thurmond and his Dixiecrats, the rabbi spoke in favor of Hubert Humphrey and integration in front of his congregation. When Ralph Bunche negotiated an armistice between Israel and Egypt under United Nations auspices, ending the war for independence, Epstein recounted Bunche's life story, emphasizing the American's role as a black man favoring brotherhood and "racial unity."[18]

As the civil rights struggle heightened during the early 1960s, some Southerners advocated equal rights to African Americans to attract Northern businesses and tourists who might reject the South because of its racism. Such a position would also tie blacks to the region as a work force. Epstein, along with other moderates—like *Atlanta Constitution* editor Ralph McGill—supported equal rights and economic opportunities because everyone deserved just treatment regardless of race or religion. It was not only the legal position after the Supreme Court declared segregation unconstitutional, it was also the right position. As early as 1963, Epstein informed his congregants that Israel, a continuing trade partner with South Africa, "cannot accept apartheid" in that country. We live in challenging, revolutionary times, the rabbi stated. People's desires for freedom coincided with Judaism's ideal of justice. Before God there is no privileged group; "only man." When President John F. Kennedy was assassinated, the rabbi's Friday night sermon denounced segregation as defiance of law and order. While many in the South advocated the closing of the public schools and the opening of private academies, Epstein stated that people must obey Supreme Court edicts, including *Brown v. Board of Education of Topeka, Kansas,* or anarchy would reign. He also denounced those who used religious arguments and parochial schools to halt integration in 1959. The Selma to Montgomery march led by Martin Luther King, Jr., to obtain voting rights was contrasted with the Gemini space flights to illustrate humanity's failures and grandeur. President Lyndon B. Johnson's "War on Poverty" was naturally seen as part of Judaism's "Millenial War." Epstein opposed Republican gubernatorial candidate Howard "Bo" Callaway and others who rejected Johnson's foreign aid and civil rights policies.

Jewish congregants and congregations throughout the South limited rabbinical freedom to speak out on controversial issues. They were fearful of their positions and afraid of an anti-Semitic reaction. Rabbi Epstein declared it a right and a duty for the clergy to define right and wrong on political issues when those issues were infused with moral imperatives. Epstein interpreted religion as a system of beliefs and practices "designed to unite people in love of God and through it, in love with each other," whereas politics was a "system thru which people regulated [their] relationship with each other." The latter elucidated "conditions under which people live." Thus, religion and politics were interrelated.

In 1966 incumbent Charles Weltner refused to run for Congress from the Fifth District because the Georgia Democratic Party had as a rule the endorsement of the other candidates on the slate. Weltner refused to support Lester Maddox's brand of racism even tacitly. Weltner's stand was singled out by Epstein as a meaningful gesture against a "symbol of hate." The rabbi advised that the greatest crime of the German people and of Pope Pius XII was "silence" in the face of Nazi atrocities. Jews must not be silent with reference to the black civil rights struggle. They had to be outspoken in their cries for brotherhood.

During the mid 1960s, events occurred that made it more difficult to support the civil rights movement. The riots or rebellions (according to different perspectives) during the summers in the cities were hard for many people to understand. Rabbi Epstein advised a thoughtful approach to a complex situation. Whereas deliberate and wanton destruction of property was not good, people did not live by bread alone. "Violence, murder, pillage, destruction" he recognized as the result of a "struggle" for "dignity . . . opportunity . . . equality." The riots were caused by a lack of progress in the provision of quality education, jobs, and housing. Whites had to accept sacrifices—higher taxes and open housing—because without such sacrifice there would not be full freedom for all. When black anti-Semitism rose during the late 1960s, the rabbi pointed out how easy it was to use Jews as scapegoats. Jews had to be aware of intergroup conflict, but they should also maintain their role in the forefront of social reform. In requesting his congregation to observe the *yahrzeit,* or anniversary of the death of Martin Luther King, Jr., Epstein defined freedom as working together to benefit others. On the death of Jacob Rothschild, rabbi of The Temple, Mayor Maynard Jackson asked Rabbi Epstein to accept the former's place on Atlanta's Community Relations Committee. A black mayor thus recognized the role of an immigrant rabbi as more than just a silent observer in the civil rights movement. He could have, instead, chosen Rothschild's successor and the symbolic leader of the German Reform Jews for this "Jewish seat," but he chose Harry Epstein. Epstein neither marched nor demonstrated. He did not take a national or even a statewide role in a civil rights organization. His was just one of many unsung voices advocating thought, moderation, and equal rights.

From the perspective of the 1990s it is difficult to think of Harry Epstein's positions as anything more than rather mundane. They clearly fit into the mold of moderate, progressive middle-class mentality. Yet, his group of mid-level leaders, little treated by historians, may have contributed substantially in swaying public opinion in a region dominated by reactionary voices. He was a member of a minority group counseling dissent from the most-notable local mores. His ideas were consistent and rooted in his sense of Judaism and what it is to be a human being.

Recent biographies of two Reform rabbis whose careers overlapped that of Epstein, Morris Newfield of Birmingham and Jacob Rothschild of Atlanta, point to substantial interaction between these men and Christian clergy and lay leaders as being critical to their social thought. Newfield was dramatically influenced by Social Gospel ministers who reinforced his European experiences. He subsequently emerged as a major force for social reform and the delivery of social services, although his fear of an anti-Semitic reaction limited him in more controversial areas. Interaction with Southern black and white integrationists informed Rothschild's position in the area of race relations, although his intellectual underpinnings were formed largely in the Pittsburgh Jewish community.

Inasmuch as Epstein spent virtually his entire adult life in the South, it is surprising to note the seeming lack of influence that the Christian clergy and general community exerted on him. Active in the National Conference of Christians and Jews, he did not form close relationships with his Christian counterparts. Although he quoted such individuals as Harry Emerson Fosdick in his sermons, these citations were used in support of his own ideas. Gentile thinkers and experience outside of his Jewish milieu, beyond his secular studies—which, as has been shown, were frequently career reinforcing—did not have a noticeable impact. He was involved with community issues, but on a limited scale. He was influenced by and participated in the civil rights struggle for blacks, but not any more or less than he might have been had he lived in the North. In many ways then, the Southern environment neither significantly expanded nor limited Epstein's spheres of action or thought. His were the perceptions of the pulpit and of the denomination.

Nonetheless, Epstein's residence in the South probably exerted a more-subtle influence. Had he lived in a major center of Jewish population with numerous competing individuals and institutions, he might have been a leader, but he would have been one of many. Possibly, his career would have resembled more his father's, in that he might have been ultimately recognized as dean of the city's Conservative or Orthodox rabbis. Then, too, he might have held higher positions in national organizations as a result of the power of the community and his more-direct contact with other leaders. Life and potential were different for an individual forging a career outside of the Philadelphia–New York–Chicago axis. Jews and their population centers were diffuse, and there were relatively few rabbis. Consequently, the reputation of a leader like Epstein could spread, and he could be called on to serve as a model for an entire region. Yet, the area might be viewed as provincial and might not have the numbers to establish national authority. Ironically, Epstein's Atlanta sojourn may have made him both more and less significant.

Stemming from the 1886 Pittsburgh Platform's emphasis on social ethics and representing congregations demographically similar to their Protestant counterparts, Reform rabbis would have been far more likely to associate with Social Gospel ministers and causes during the 1890s and early-twentieth century than the small number of Orthodox rabbis in the region. The latter would have been concerned with the needs of a new immigrant community of which they were a part. Again during the 1940s and into the heyday of the Civil Rights movement, the few Southern rabbis who were active and more deeply involved were from the Reform movement. Orthodox and Conservative rabbis had different priorities, especially the maintenance of at least a modicum of tradition and Zionism. Secular social reforms could be important causes for the Conservative rabbinate, but these causes were clearly of an extracurricular mold. Being accepted and being a part of the general community, to the extent of attempting to change it, was clearly secondary when viewed by rabbis who feared for the very survival of Judaism and of the Jewish people.

6

The World of Ideas

Nonetheless, Rabbi Epstein's social commitment was grounded in a well-thought-out, logical worldview. His worldview, in turn, was based on his family background and experience, his education, and his personality. Here was a very secure individual who knew how and why to lead, and who would alter methods without compromising fundamental beliefs.

A discussion of Epstein's concept of religion is a logical place to begin to understand his worldview. The rabbi defined religion in several ways in accordance with the lesson he was attempting to impart. "Religion," he wrote, "is a yearning for the highest good, the greatest beauty, the highest truth." In one of his early radio messages, Epstein stated that religion was a civilizing and humanizing force on society. It encouraged help for others in need, and it nurtured art, education, science, philosophy, a daily business ethic, and medicine. "All religions reflected to some extent the knowledge of times in which they flourished, and that the real underlying purpose of religion should be the practical betterment of humanity, the advancement of civilization in the best sense of the word."[1]

Had religion failed to deter World War I and its carnage, as some maintained? No, according to Epstein; religion had not been tried. It "does not work automatically. To be effective [it] must be accepted and followed." In a broader sense, "religion is life, and is to be defined in terms of life . . . our daily life should be such that we are ever occupied with doing justice, loving mercy, and walking humbly before God." Religion was like a telescope. It was not so much to be looked at as to be looked through. The "acid test of religion," he articulated at a later date, was its "validity and usefulness [in] shaping and moulding human life." Religion made life "nobler" by setting higher goals. It was not an escape, but rather a guide, inspiration, and influence on daily life. Religion was at the root of ethics, and, in fact, there could be no ethics without it. When ethics is not grounded in religion, it may be compromised to expediency. But when based on religion, which, it follows, relies on God through conviction and faith, backsliding would not be countenanced.

Harry Epstein's perception of religion, then, was based on several interlocking concepts, including the relationship between individuals and that between individuals and God. Religion, the rabbi made clear, was "man's progressive quest to express and interpret the greatest and most inclusive of all relationships to the universe, to himself, to his fellow man, to the power above, over, beyond and within himself." Since, to Epstein at least in theory, there was no distinction drawn between the spiritual and the profane, between principle and practice, these relationships were not really multiple. Rather, they were different manifestations of one. Religion had to be applied to daily activities and to an individual's interaction with other individuals. People could not be contented unless they were striving to improve daily life and to attain higher personal horizons. One could not achieve success through material advancement. Epstein defined success as "what one is" as measured by "love, friendship, companionship . . . family, faith . . . a good name, character, convictions . . . a good conscience, integrity." Epstein constantly counterposed idealism with materialism. Even and perhaps especially to his affluent congregants, the latter never triumphed.[2]

The other side of the interrelational equation involved God. Whereas religion was predicated on individuals doing good toward others, that aspect was not all there was to religion. Individuals could perform good deeds, but their actions had to be based on a belief in God. In fact, "the root of goodness is God," the rabbi quipped. The example of God encourages good behavior, and those who attempt to know God act out their conceptions of his goodness. The latter involves the Jewish ethical precepts of Kiddush HaShem and Chillul HaShem—the transmission of holiness through daily living and the patterning of one's life after God. Those who would follow these precepts would act in a fashion that they believe God would want them to act. Their actions would virtually illustrate proof, in part, of God's existence and of God's values. To Epstein, the "Jewish mission," in particular, was proclaiming "the kingdom of God on Earth."[3]

The right to question God, Epstein believed, was at the heart of Jewish "ethical teaching." When one questioned, however, one also had the responsibility to wait for an answer and to learn. Yet, this questioning was a two-way street. God questioned humanity also through history. History was a major part of Rabbi Epstein's cosmology. It assumed an almost organic quality influenced in part by the positive historicism of Zacharias Frankel. Frankel's approach used history as a source of continuous revelation of both God's design and human experience. Thus, history was not important in and of itself, but as a starting point for the future, a gauge of trends, and a foundation for progress. From a greater knowledge of and appreciation for the past, an individual or a group would gain strength to strive for a higher level of accomplishment. Ignoring one's past opened the hazard of destroying one's distinctiveness, of losing touch with one's cultural identity.[4]

During the late 1920s, at a time when it seemed to many that science and technology were in a position to conquer all challenges, Rabbi Epstein asked rhetorically, "Why go back?" His answer was that the Torah taught that "the Jew's progress is in his regress!" The Jew should "go along in the ranks of progress . . . [but also draw] a battlement [of Jewish spirit] around himself." Progress could thus be had in a meaningful fashion within traditions. The lesson of history taught that nations rose and fell when their "rush for civilization, in [their] drive for progress . . . [they did not] make a fortress about [their] cultural center with which to keep in bounds . . . ." "A Jew's progress," he continued, "is in that he continually retains in his memory the great ancestors of his religion." Progress was to be gradually accrued as God's majesty slowly unfolded through history.

The lessons of history were many, and Epstein used historical examples in more sermons and speeches than perhaps any other explanatory tool. From history the Jews learned about the moral power of God and of God's purpose. History offered a guide for current actions and a base on which to make decisions. It helped Jews compare and contrast themselves with other religions and cultures to discern signs of strength and weakness. Archaeology and biblical criticism supported the Bible as a book of parables and provided evidence of Jewish history. In the face of Nazism, history made people remember past triumphs and the passing nature of despotism so that they could remain optimistic and combat despair. When history taught the harshness of life, it offered the capacity for relief through humor and self-criticism. History could also "rank as a vital part of faith." In his master's thesis, Epstein showed how it could be used to prove the existence of God. The God of Jewish history could be a God of creation and justice, but also a God of retribution against the enemies of the Jews.[5]

Epstein's perception of evolution was integrated with his concept of history. As history was an unfolding saga opening new meanings to historical Judaism, so, too, evolution followed God's ever unfolding pattern of life. Epstein interpreted Henri Bergson's "creative evolution" as an inner life force within matter. God created nature in a certain, uniform method. Natural laws were "not forces nor powers," but merely observed uniformities. Epstein defined biological evolution as virtually synonymous with development; "orderly, progressive changes. . . . in the direction of greater complexity and a higher degree of organization." Humanity is "the crowning masterpiece of Nature's evolutionary methods . . . a divine achievement." Thus, while Christian fundamentalists and modernists fought these questions in churches, in the classrooms, and in the courts, Epstein took his stand with those who might be called moderates who saw no conflict between religion and evolution. These individuals sought to remain within the churches while coming to grips with newly revealed/observed knowledge. The rabbi believed, too, that evolution helped religious people understand the world by enlarging their vision. Just like nature, Judaism must not remain static. It had to adjust to changing environments while maintaining cognizance of historically important moral lessons. Could the theories of evolution answer all questions regarding life? No, it "has not explained what life is or how it began, nor how it reproduces itself, nor how growth and assimilation take place, nor why there is a struggle for existence, nor how and why variations occur, nor even how species change into one another; nor has it explained that which is most important of all, the origin and nature of consciousness." These are questions that remain for philosophy grounded on religion. Reading from history, one of Epstein's answers implied, one learned that survival did not depend on brute force, but instead on the "ability to associate and work together harmoniously." "The dominant principle of social life" was that life was "not a struggle for existence"; it was a "struggle for cooperation." Philosophically, Epstein would not have felt uncomfortable in the camp of the Social Gospel adherents of the late nineteenth and early twentieth centuries, or with the liberal Christian clergy of his own era. His ideas were also well within the mainstream of American Jewish thought.[6]

Too, like many of his Christian counterparts and Jewish colleagues, he believed that, whereas God created the universe, human beings had been granted free will. Actually, Epstein considered human beings to be "cocreators" with God as a result of this freedom. Although in line with progressive rabbis, he was probably venturing beyond any but the most liberal Christian clergy. God, Epstein held, had not created a perfect world. Creation was a continuous process. God provided humanity with a guide to nurture greater perfection in the God-given environment. Human beings had to have faith in God, but God also had to have faith in humanity. With God and humanity as partners, human beings had the responsibility of not leaving problems up to God to solve. People had to actualize their religious faith through moral deeds. Faith was more than a simple expression toward God. It had to be reflected in good works mirroring a "God of justice, rights, peace, brotherhood, goodness, mercy." "The highest kind of freedom" Epstein specified as "that wherein one comes to recognize one's right and obligation to make one's choices on an ethical or spiritual level." Freedom existed within a societal structure. The truly free person, thus, lived with other people bound by morally just laws. God had created human beings with the ability to do good or evil. This was the Enlightenment's tabula rasa. It was up to humanity to make the correct choices. Why had God allowed the existence of evil? Without it human beings really would not have had freedom to choose. Illustrating his faith in humanity by allowing people this freedom, God became dependent on them. Whether or not God is remote, or if the world is dark or light, depended on people's actions.[7]

God's gift of free will to humanity paralleled and complemented the political concept of democracy in Rabbi Epstein's moral universe. The goal of both religion and democracy was the "sanctity of human life." This sanctity reached fruition through the nurturing of the individual's personality. "God's task is the making of man," Epstein averred. "The American task is the sanctification of man." During the 1930s and 1940s, the rabbi gave a series of Passover sermons that emphasized freedom in opposition to fascism. In these sermons he stressed that freedom was a spirit, a feeling within individuals to act as they thought correct. Freedom meant that one was free from being a servant to others. One was free to think, to practice God's will, to help others, and to make one's choices on an ethical basis.[8]

The individual could only be free as a part of the group. This relationship existed because the "greatest satisfaction in life lies in the feeling of attachment or belonging to some individual, family, group or country . . . none of us can live alone and for ourselves. [We] must have someone to share with." In the mid 1960s, Epstein defined "Jewish values in western civilization" through four essential concepts: God, democracy, reverence for life, and the peaceful unity of humanity through these ideals. He saw the Jewish regard for the individual within society as the foundation of America. Epstein viewed democracy as the high point of the evolution of the human personality. It signified the victory of right over might. As such, it offered hope to society and a bastion of religion. Epstein summarized his beliefs concerning freedom to a sisterhood institute in 1974. "In successive stages man seeks to be free—free as a human being; free to live as an individual; free as a people; free to create values and our tradition sums up this entire process in one word—redemption." In a remarkably simple fashion, mirroring the thoughts of Louis Brandeis, and typical of the rabbi's generation in the pulpit, Epstein thus synthesized the meeting of a homogenized Jewish thought with Americanism.

Although religion and democracy were mutually reinforcing instruments, religion had several tools of its own that added to its institutional strength. One such tool was prayer. Prayer fulfilled numerous functions, from Rabbi Epstein's perspective. It purified the individual when it was directed at the recognition of the higher role of God and the humanity of the individual. As a "self preached sermon," it involved thought and meditation on God, life and one's function in life. Prayer "brings home needed lessons" of morality. It kept religion and ethical teachings in people's minds and encouraged them to practice beliefs through positive actions. Prayer was both a spiritual and an intellectual experience. People needed prayer when they were insecure and when they were contented. It provided strength even as it forced them to ask questions of themselves. When one prays one wrestles between "conscience and temptation." If the individual is to win, he or she had to become sanctified—had to strive for perfection.[9]

Although one of Judaism's major contributions to humanity was the concept of a prayer book and prayers that all could recite, as opposed to those reserved for the priests, organized group prayer had special significance. The standardization of communal worship included truths to be rehearsed "so we won't overlook things." It prepared people for daily trials and helped them appreciate everyday occurrences. The order of the service assisted people in structuring their thoughts. Most importantly, communal worship offered the benefits of "spiritual fellowship," in which individuals would feel that they were part of a whole. When the scene of prayer, the synagogue, or church, then, becomes "a community house" in which "we are weighed down with the burden of the whole people," the worshippers realized that the universe was more important than the individual. One came to synagogue to worship in order to find "communion with God" and to create "a spiritual ideal" so that one can better strive for "righteousness and justice."

Likewise, the celebration of holidays did more than provide the "meaning and lessons" of the particular event. Holidays were "the moral mile-stones on our path of life . . . they bid us pause a while amidst the hubbub and humdrum of our life, stop, think, refreshen ourselves, then go on higher." Holidays, along with other occasions for communal prayer, add meaning to daily existence. One should examine the outward form of the ceremonial act to appreciate what the act means and conveys. Observance in this fashion offered a way of life, a learning instrument, a sense of participation in a historical experience, a feeling of fellowship, an art form, discipine, and a survival mechanism. Harry Epstein offered a bulwark for outward individual and group observance acceptable to the middle class in an era when many stopped practicing ceremonies that were normative in the old world.

Whereas Epstein equated the synagogue with the "heart of Jewry," the rabbi was at the heart of his synagogue. Although lay people often viewed the preaching of a sermon as a critical responsibility of the rabbi, Epstein did not consider this task to be extremely significant. To him, the "sermon has to answer a question. Hopefully it answers a question that someone asks, but sometimes it answers a question that no one asks." A good sermon made congregants think and analyze the world around them. Epstein, in practice, spent much time in the development of his sermons. He realized that in the modern era the sermon could be used for instruction, to stimulate loyalty to tradition, and to identify current Jewish and world problems. He read and took notes extensively. He would first thoroughly detail a subject, specifying important anecdotes, statistics, and quotations, and then compose an outline version on small notepaper. In his sermons Epstein quoted the Bible, the Talmud, and other Jewish sources, used frequent comparison with other religions and cultures (the Greeks in particular), made extensive reference to literature, and often took lessons from history. Sermons were well thought out, delivered, and received. In Epstein's hands, they became one of many educational tools helping the rabbi perform his more-important tasks. It was the rabbi who gave the synagogue character and personality. A teacher and guide, the rabbi set the goals and objectives of the congregation. The rabbi could not "make" Jews, but he could nurture them. Certainly, the sermon helped in these functions. Yet, according to Rabbi Epstein, "the worth of the rabbi . . . is to be gauged not so much by what he says as by what he achieves in the development of a wholesome Jewish community life."

Epstein's two favorite and most-memorable sermons were the ones he preached when he and his congregants were informed of the Yom Kippur attack on Israel, actually during the holiday ceremony, and his farewell address, which was interrupted and resumed as he tried to control his emotions. Thus, the man who emphasized the intellect recognized the equality of heartfelt feelings in the process of spiritual awakening, unity, and commitment.[10]

In his inaugural and sermons at B'nai Emunah in Tulsa and at Atlanta's Ahavath Achim, Epstein related the modern-day rabbi's role to that of the ancient kings and priests. Like them, he had to be friendly, peaceful, and compassionate and, at the same time, show righteous indignation when criticizing faults. Since the Talmudic era when learned rabbis interpreted God's words and intent in the Bible, the rabbis were the real rulers. The rabbi must be one with the people and yet be over the people according to the situation. Circumstances usually dictated that the rabbi act as "disturber of peace." If the rabbi and congregation became too complacent with their lot, something was amiss.

Constant searching for improvement was clearly one of Epstein's objectives. It was difficult to be a leader, and a rabbi in particular. The rabbi was confronted with many trials. He was subject to emotional strain. He had to provide counsel to congregants on daily problems. He frequently became embroiled in contentious issues in which his opinions were not necessarily valued, and, nonetheless, he had to stand firm in the face of pressure. The leader's "ultimate position and authority" depended on the character of the group that he represented. One of the leader's greatest dangers was that his ideals and values would be diluted by his followers. The leader could be "spokesman for his people if they appreciate the ideals which he represents." He could also be a leader without a following.

In 1962, Epstein responded to an article in the *Saturday Evening Post* entitled "Why I quit the ministry" with a sermon on "Why one stays in the ministry." He stated that he empathized with the former minister. Every minister was "often discouraged" because the majority of the congregational members refused to care about God or humanity. The ministry, too, was a lonely profession. No one understood the work involved, and the minister was one of a kind in the congregation. One got frustrated with a failure to accomplish goals and the recognition that a religious body was far from a "club for saints . . . [but rather a] clinic for spiritually sick." Yet, the rabbi had to "strive and never quit." He had to remain optimistic even as he held his own counsel, knowing that his function had substantial importance to the well-being of his people. If the rabbi had been dedicated to God and goodness, if he supported his convictions so that his congregation imbibed his sense of idealism, then his reward would be found in the life and character of his congregation. If Judaism was vital because it was lived and taught, if the attachment to Judaism had grown, then the rabbi had had a "glorious and productive career." An Epstein informed a radio audience in 1952, "All lives influence us—good or bad. We all live by example. . . . Blessed are they whose goodness and integrity serve as a source of blessing and as an ideal to be followed." So, too, would Rabbi Epstein's ideal rabbi be blessed.

For two decades Epstein performed the additional rabbinic role of judge. The few records of cases surviving illustrate the specifically Jewish values Epstein brought to the task. In two of the cases the court decided against the plaintiffs, but it forced the innocent party in one instance to pay court expenses and legal fees, and, in the other, to give the plaintiff fifteen dollars in order to be able to leave Atlanta. The innocent were wealthier individuals "bound in justice" to assist those less fortunate. Another case over an insurance check became difficult to adjudicate. The only reasonable solution determinable was that the individual less in the right (or more in the wrong!) had to donate twenty-five dollars to the United Hebrew School. The charity would be the beneficiary in a situation that two friends should have worked out among themselves.[11]

A final illustration was an instance not brought before the arbitration court. Rabbi Epstein was informed about a man who apparently had abandoned his wife and family in a very unseemly fashion. Epstein wrote to the man, raising the principle of "Chillul HaShem" and urging the man to move back with his wife at least "for appearance's sake." This step would prevent her from being "made the laughing-stock of her friends, her family, and the community in which she lives." A meeting was requested between the man and the rabbi to "reach at certain decisions that will be for the best for all concerned." Rabbinic justice was clearly tempered by a desire for order and harmony, social responsibility and fair play. Community responsibility involved taking care of those even in the wrong.

Much of what has been written here concerning Harry Epstein's worldview with regard to religion could be applied in his thought to most religions with an ethical basis. He respected other religions and believed that they served an important function so long as their adherents upheld philosophy through practice. All religions came from the same source and attempted to answer the same questions. Nonetheless, Epstein was not a universalist who believed that all religions were equal and that the ultimate triumph would come with the elimination of denominational differences. Epstein was a particularist and a pluralist. He was convinced of the superiority of Judaism and the need to accept religious diversity. While calling on everyone to avoid intolerance, Epstein argued that Judaism was the supremely significant faith "not merely for us but for all mankind." Judaism had overcome ancient paganism, was the "mother faith" for both Christianity and Islam, and served as a "powerful factor" in these philosophies and religions.[12]

Judaism surpassed the other religions historically since no other improved on the message of "social righteousness" of the Hebrew Prophets. "Is not Jewish preachment of social redemption by justice and integrity superior," he asked, "to the Christian doctrine of salvation by faith in Christ as Lord and Saviour?" Had not Judaism "proved its survival value throughout the millenia" by its ability to adjust? Judaism differed from other religions in that it was two-dimensional. It related both person to person and the individual to God. It interpreted the role of the Prophets at variance with Christians. The Prophets, according to the Jews, Epstein maintained, did not foretell the future. Instead, they acted as spokesmen for God's word. They dealt with the contemporary world and daily living.

Neither did Jews deal with miracles in the same fashion as others. Such phenomena could not be invoked as decisive evidence of God among Jews, but rather as incidents from which one could learn important lessons. All religions had an ideal of God, but ceremony and ritual made each distinctive, and these forms of observance played a larger role in Judaism than they did in other religions.

From a positive perspective, Judaism was "a practical, an ethical discipline, a mental and spiritual striving, and an attitude of confidence in the possibilities of men and women." It did "not despise the body, but addresses itself to the soul." It was more than Jewish holidays, Jewish charity, and Jewish organizations. The ultimate goal of Judaism was righteousness. Jews actively strove for unity of actions and thoughts, faith in God, acceptance of the Torah, recognition of a prophetic "moral passion," renewal and continuity of Jewish historical experience, the practice of a way of life, and the espousal of certain values. Jews, stated Rabbi Epstein, were "guardians and trustees of this our tradition." They were not threatened by science. They learned from it and grew in their beliefs and understanding. Their "holidays celebrate universal human aspirations." They did not force their religion on others, but they did believe in a "united humanity." They did not spend their time worrying about heaven and hell, but they did believe that evil was made—or unmade—by people. What did Judaism offer its adherents? Epstein responded: a way to live with others and God, stability, and a purpose to live for, and an "ideal pattern." Judaism was not just ethics, philosophy, or theology. It was "the way of truth, justice and happiness."[13]

As a result of their distinctiveness and their role as messengers of righteousness, it was incumbent on Jews not to assimilate. Epstein believed that people assimilated because they did not want to be different. And yet, he surmised, people were not afraid of being singled out if they were beautiful or brilliant. Thus, they could be distinctive if traits associated with their culture were recognized and viewed positively by the society. Then, Jews would accept their positions in a pluralistic environment if they were accepted as, and accepted themselves as bearers of a great tradition who were dedicated servants of society with values to contribute to the general good. This mission would have to be communicated to others. Just as critically when dealing with the matter of assimilation, the Jews themselves would have to be made proud of their uniqueness through education. To assure continued survival, Jews should learn about their heritage and live as committed followers of religious practice and values. They must share a "fire of enthusiasm" with their fellow congregants.[14]

Such a spirit would lead Jews to join educational programs, to participate in services, and to further support patterned behavior. Jewish life as a people was "determined by our loyalty to Judaism through the Synagogue." If Jews lost their identity and their sense of community as a minority, they would be swept away with the tide, and their unique contributions would be lost. Epstein was cognizant of the problem facing Jews in America. America is a voluntaristic society allowing substantial freedom and encouraging acceptance through integration into society—the melting pot ideal. When one is neither forced, nor isolated, it is relatively easier to accept such practices as the celebration of Christmas and Easter, virtual national holidays devoid of religious connotation that become a part of what church historians call "civil religion," than to maintain a separate identity and culture.

During one frustrating week in 1970, a congregant wished the rabbi a happy Easter. Another questioned the relevance of Jewish education and complained about too much Hebrew school. Repeatedly, the rabbi counseled pride, greater commitment—not less— and more knowledge through education—not less. One should not simply be a Jew. One should strive to be a modern Jew. With that striving, the relevance and meaning of the religion would become evident. Harry Epstein filled the role of ethnic leader advocating the cultural pluralism of Horace Kallen.

While he admonished Jews to remain within the faith and defined Judaism as separate from and superior to other religions, he also found himself in the midst of the debate over divisions within Judaism itself. Distinctions seemed to follow distinctiveness, as Epstein attempted to delineate his and his fellow's place in the world. The rabbi's images of the different forms of Jewish practice and belief must be placed in the context of his career and background. It will be recalled that Epstein came from a family that was strictly Orthodox, but one that made some allowances for modernity. The acceptance of change was compounded with his yeshiva and secular educations and with his concept of Talmudic, or rabbinic, Judaism. The latter was based on the precept that the Bible had to be interpreted. The Babylonian and Jerusalem rabbis had performed this task early in the common era in what became the Talmud and other commentaries. In turn, these commentaries had been expanded and analyzed during the Middle Ages. Contemporary Jews were expected to follow these expositions as opposed to the original scriptures. Those Jews, like Epstein, who accepted this position found support for the rabbinic role as expositor of biblical and divine messages. The rabbi was delegated the authority, then, to apply Talmudic lessons to contemporary circumstances.

After a brief stay at an Orthodox congregation in Tulsa, Epstein had journeyed to a synagogue in Atlanta that was equally Orthodox, but that had sought an American rabbi who could entice the participation of the Americanized generation. His program from the onset involved compromising traditional ceremonies while attempting to maintain the essential ingredients of Orthodox belief as he applied them. This program was Talmudic Judaism in the contemporary setting. By 1952, Epstein and his congregation actualized the tendencies of modern Orthodoxy by formally affiliating with the Conservative United Synagogue of America organization.

In a broad sense, regardless of the existence of national bodies for the four branches of Judaism, American Jewry is governed on a congregational basis. Congregations and rabbis are essentially autonomous. Whether Ahavath Achim chose to call itself Orthodox or Conservative, it tended to create its own practices, influenced by national trends, and, consequently, influencing those trends. Even as Epstein defined, compared, and contrasted Judaism's different arms, like contemporary Joseph Lookstein, he actually felt more comfortable with the nomenclature "traditional," a more-accurate term that reflected the basic continuity throughout Epstein's rabbinical career.[15]

As might be expected, Rabbi Epstein's definitions corresponded to some extent with his changing affiliations and the periods of his career. During the 1930s, ignoring Conservatism entirely (Atlanta lacked a Conservative congregation, and it was thus not in contention for power), Epstein declared that Reform and Orthodox shared fundamentally similar ideas. As a proponent of modern Orthodoxy, he suggested that, whereas formerly there had been differences in observance, now these differences had lessened. Even Orthodox congregations had adopted mixed seating and English sermons. Both also recognized that Judaism was "sick." They parted company, however, with their therapy. The Orthodox attempted to treat

the disease with medication for the patient. They encouraged observance, recognized the beauty of Hebrew even as they incorporated
English responsive readings, and revived Judaism by preserving the
meaning of customs. Reform, on the other hand, sought to combat
the ills of Judaism by denaturing the faith. The Reformers, Epstein
averred, rejected Zionism, rejected Hebrew usage, and rejected the
meaning as well as the trappings of ritual, so that little Jewish indi-
viduality remained and differences were minimal between a Reform
temple and a Unitarian church. Reform to Epstein was synonymous
with assimilation. With its "abstract universal values" and especially
its rejection of Zionism (which Epstein virtually equated with Judaism), Reform was doomed to stagnation. Even worse, it could contribute to the demise of Judaism as an identifiable religious entity.[16]

During the early 1950s, Conservatism came to the fore in Epstein's mind, and his attitude toward Orthodox and Reform underwent transformation. Now, the rabbi believed that the Orthodox
lived in the past and ignored American conditions. Orthodoxy
"holds rigidly to the practices of the law." As "strict traditionalists,"
the followers of Orthodoxy believed that the Talmud and the Torah
were divinely inspired and were thus not subject to inquiry. The
"form was as important as the reason." When Epstein reviewed
Herman Wouk's *This Is My God* before a Macon congregation in
1960, he rejected what he viewed as Wouk's apologia for Orthodoxy's static God with "no prophetic vision." Epstein actually appeared to be more tolerant of Reform Judaism. Reform had simply
"abandoned most of the ancient ritual" as it accepted the triumph
of reason and "the results of modern critical scholarship."

Epstein now defined Conservative Judaism much as he had previously defined modern Orthodoxy. Conservatives were the "modern
traditionalists," whose aim was the preservation in America of the
knowledge and practices of "Historical Judaism as expounded by
Prophets, sages, and rabbis throughout the ages." Never static, Conservative Judaism represented the "evolving character of Judaism."
"Continuity and change," the "tradition of the past within the framework of the present," these were the hallmarks of Conservatism.
While Reform and Orthodox movements delineated tradition as
ready-made, with the one accepting it and the other rejecting it,
Conservative Judaism adapted it into a "dynamic concept" of the
"law of growth and development."[17]

Three additional factors may have had bearing on his perceptions.

A significant contingent of ultra-Orthodox rabbis settled in America as they escaped Hitler's tentacles during the Holocaust and shortly after World War II. Historians of Orthodox Judaism have indicated that these individuals brought an uncompromising brand of Orthodox cultural baggage with them, as they frequently settled in relatively ghettoized districts of New York City, its proximate boroughs, and elsewhere. They exerted a profound impact on national Orthodoxy, swinging it away from modernity and toward strict constructionism. In 1954 the Agudath HaRabbanim reiterated its earlier rejection of cooperation with followers of Conservatism and Reform Judaism. While there is no record of the impact of this situation on Rabbi Epstein, it may be surmised that he may have perceived a limited future for modern Orthodoxy on the national level. Such trends could have been seen as having a potentially stifling influence on his congregation, and the roles he expected to play and looked forward to congregants performing in the national arena.[18]

Another consideration was his relationship with other rabbis in the Atlanta community. It was not unusual for new Orthodox rabbis coming into a small city to experience friction with older, more Orthodox, less assimilated rabbis. The spark of the conflict was usually control of the lucrative kosher butcher supervision. But the ultimate source was probably competition for respect, power, and prestige. The elders did not want their roles challenged by upstarts and, in some cases, may even have been afraid of comparisons and of losing members to new methods and a new personality. The circumstances in Atlanta illustrate a variation on this pattern.

Tobias Geffen had been Congregation Shearith Israel's rabbi for almost twenty years when Epstein arrived in 1928. Shearith Israel was not dramatically different in ritual from Ahavath Achim during the 1920s, and, frequently, families held joint memberships in the two synagogues. The greater difference was represented by a lower level of assimilation and the lower socioeconomic status of the Shearith Israel clientele. Geffen was considered the outstanding rabbinic authority of the city. Intellectually, he actually lived within the European milieu, writing learned articles for European Jewish journals, speaking Yiddish, and opposing accommodationism. When Harry Epstein arrived in Atlanta, and for years thereafter, according to Epstein, Rabbi Geffen remained cool to him, only to apologize years later. One can conjecture that Epstein, even with his solid credentials and family ties, presented a challenge to the older

man. Harry Epstein's youth and his attractiveness as a preacher and
a leader could only further draw away congregants and prestige.
Combating the new activities and style, or standing in comparison
with them, would be hard for Rabbi Geffen. At any rate, Geffen
probably would have rejected the new approach and even perhaps
the need for such outreach.[19]

Rabbi Epstein seems to have gained the respect of the Reform
rabbis more readily than that of the Orthodox leader. David Marx
and Jacob Rothschild tended to work with different individuals and
had different agendas than Epstein. Still Epstein shared the podium
on important occasions with all three counterparts and cooperated
on social service efforts in behalf of the community. Yet, even
though Marx was an ardent anti-Zionist, and Epstein was patroniz-
ing toward the Reform rabbis' lack of Hebrew and Jewish knowledge, Epstein seems to have accepted the Reformers because he
recognized the rationale for their positions vis-à-vis Jewish ceremony. This is not to say that Epstein was receptive to, or agreed
with, their conclusions and methods, but rather that he understood
their logic as an extension of certain strains of Jewish tradition.

Finally, his father's experience may have been acting as a guide-
post. According to a friend—a Chicago rabbinic colleague and historian of the Hebrew Theological College, Leonard Mishkin—
Ephraim Epstein, a man of aristocratic bearing in the best sense
himself, presided over a most prestigious and aristocratic congregation of Chicago Orthodoxy from about 1911 to 1939. By the latter
date, the young people were moving away from the Lawndale area,
away from the congregation, and away from Orthodoxy and observance. Ephraim Epstein's congregation dwindled in membership
even though he was an acknowledged giant of his community who
had sought their input.[20]

What, then, was the impact of these reference points on Epstein's
attitudes toward the other modes of Judaism? Again, one must resort
to conjecture, given the lack of written sources. He obviously witnessed a local example of the nature and results of an apparently
stultifying Orthodoxy. He also saw an illustration of an individual
involved in community activities, but whose congregation was on
the decline numerically and in relation to commitment and knowledge. Rothschild breathed new life into The Temple when he succeeded Marx to the pulpit. Although they were minor from
Epstein's perspective, he even reintroduced certain rituals. The

membership and involvement of The Temple group dramatically increased accordingly. Thus, Epstein's march down the middle of the road, merging innovative techniques with tradition and social action, and his gradual move toward Conservatism were reinforced through his local observations and experiences.

Surprisingly, Epstein had little to say concerning one force that exerted a profound influence on him. He recognized Mordecai Kaplan as a seminal thinker who impacted especially on Conservative Judaism and on Epstein's views concerning the synagogue. Yet, he believed the Reconstructionists to be individuals relying overly on Jewish "folkways . . . the simple practices of Jewish people." The role of God was too pivotal for Epstein's world view to countenance such a (to him) denatured reliance on ceremonies.[21]

One of the fundamental distinctions Epstein drew between the branches of Judaism had its origins in the questions he had asked Rabbi Sher while a student in Slobodka. Epstein had queried Sher concerning the origins of faith. His early questions became the subject of his master's thesis, as they were reformulated around the issue of "religious certainty" delineated by six different Jewish schools of thought. To this day, the rabbi has not found a sufficient answer to his intellectual dilemma.

In his thesis Harry Epstein posited a spectrum of thought, from those who would accept a belief in God on faith to the extreme rationalists who would accept only ideas based on evidence and a reliance on reason. The struggle Epstein perceived was between mind and heart, empiricism and mysticism. In a characteristic conclusion, the rabbi seemed to regret that Jewish philosophy had never transcended the "scholastic stage" in that it did not benefit overly from the Enlightenment. Oppression, in essence, drove the East European community toward the legalism of the Talmud and, in some quarters, to the mysticism of the Cabala. On the other hand, the rabbi contended, religion "can never be fully understood. There is more in religion than can be in any adequate sense grasped by the mind." Judaism had to be comprehended as "a positive and historical religion" through the use of all of a person's faculties. Thus, the rabbi could accept the Reform rationalists, biblical criticism, and the concepts of the Bible story as allegory as part of Jewish theological tradition. He also could respect the mystical seeker after divine guidance.[22]

For evidence for religious certainty, Epstein and his rationalists looked to historical experience, the study of nature, and the lessons of pragmatism (visualize: if religion makes people nobler and guides them to set higher goals, then it has validity and utility). Faith was harder to pinpoint. It was "not given to scientific investigation and verification." People should inquire and seek out evidence. But they should not lose faith if they do not find it. "God's ways do not always burst clear upon our vision. We do not always find signs as proof for promised things." Still, our search must continue, and "belief must conquer in the end."[23]

Typically, Harry Epstein used different tools to emphasize his position. He compared and contrasted Greek and Jewish culture frequently, although most often during the holiday of Hanukkah, which celebrated the Israeli revolt under the Maccabee family against the Greeks. Both cultures sought the answers to life, with the Hellenic civilization relying on logic and the Hebrew culture turning to faith. To Epstein, the Greeks were limited in their vision and, to some extent, lifeless. They valued form without substance. The Jews, by contrast, saw the whole person and the entire universe. It was the Jewish people who found meaning behind surface beauty because they understood that learning and comprehension existed beyond logic.

A second tool Epstein resorted to was his virtual equation of faith with hope. At a Southeast regional Zionist meeting just after the outbreak of World War II in Europe, the rabbi referred to "the secret of Jewish survival." That secret was a "messianic . . . faith in ultimate redemption and rehabilitation." The faith would reign victorious regardless of human folly. The contemporary symbol was the Palestinian Yishuv suffering to establish a Jewish homeland. To many people, Hitler and the Holocaust challenged their beliefs in God and their faith in God and civilization. Epstein used a series of High Holiday sermons during the war to emphasize his faith in God and the meaning of humanity's relationship with God. The rabbi reiterated that God acted through people, that people must find God within themselves, and that they should act accordingly rather than using God as a scapegoat. Epstein's was not a blind faith, but one "based upon knowledge and . . . conviction born of understanding." When the Jews were liberated from the concentration camps, he noted twenty-four years later, postwar investigations indicated that they were the only group in Europe not despairing. Even amid their physical destruction, they had maintained faith and hope. Jews, according to Epstein, do not ask, "Where will it all end?" Instead they inquire, "What will be?" As he equated Zionism and Judaism, Epstein also used the establishment of Israel as historical evidence of faith. The Jewish state had translated into "salvation for hundreds of thousands" as it emerged as an act of faith and determination.

Harry Epstein was above all a man of hope. Although he lived through personal tragedies and historical horrors, his optimism never seemed to waiver. Observing discrimination abound, he believed that prejudice was not innate. It was socially conditioned and thus could be programmed out of existence. Even in death he saw hope. Rather than emphasizing it as an end, he stressed the belief that humanity can renew life. Here was the real glory: "the ability to produce a new harvest." Life is not permanent, but there is permanence to the process of recovering and rebuilding character.

Epstein's last explanation of faith can be difficult for the modern mind to accept. It will be recalled that the area of Lithuania in which he was born and first attended yeshiva in Slobodka included people who subscribed to many schools of thought. Some followed the ultra-Orthodox practices of Hassidism, and others espoused the Cabala. Although Harry Epstein was not a member of either school, he was influenced especially by the latter and came to accept it as a valid aspect of Judaism.

"In my opinion," he wrote, "mysticism is one of the greatest strongholds of religion. It brings confidence to religion. I deem mysticism as absolutely essential to religion. . . . Thus Judaism, whatever be its composition or spiritual outlook, is certainly a religion of mysticism." During the fall of 1929 he wrote a term paper on Cabala, which largely summarized his belief on the subject. He began the paper with a definition of Cabala as the "general name . . . for every kind of school of mystical interpretation" in Judaism. He traced its introduction to the thirteenth century as a reaction to the specificity of the Talmud and Mishnah. The group that emerged as Cabalists sought an inner, mysterious meaning in the Talmud essentially out of their own minds, and based on the works of authors from the first centuries of this era and on the *Zohar*. They created an imaginative religious philosophical system from their own intelligence clothed in the trappings of the sacred books and revelation, and guarded by the select initiates. Their "speculative science . . . claimed to unveil the secrets of the creation of the Divine Nature." Borrowing from the very difficult *Sefer Yetzirah,* they sought meaning in "the sounds, shapes, relative positions, and numerical values of the letters of the Hebrew alphabet." From this vantage point, the Cabalists taught that God and the world are unified and are not a duality. The *Zohar*, of unknown author and time period, uses allegory to discern the inner meaning of every word in the Bible. Among the key beliefs of the Cabalists were that all things "emanated" from God even as they remained part of God; that the kinship between God and humanity can best be expressed through the soul; and that the mystic's goal is to complete a pilgrimage toward oneness in God. Epstein viewed this definition of Cabala positively. These Jewish mystics sought the very essence of the Bible and God through what some Protestants call an "inner light," and what the rabbi delineated as "the immediate vision . . . [of] a soul alone with God." Thus, Harry Epstein accepted the mystical rejection of reason and the espousal of sense perceptions, at the same time that he supported a rational approach to practicing Judaism and dealing with daily life.[24]

This mixture and Epstein's thought process concerning the relationship between faith and reason, humanity and God can best be understood by quoting extensively from a sermon abstracted in the *Atlanta Constitution* in 1935. The sermon was one of a series offered by distinguished local clergy and was entitled "False attacks upon religion." In his submission, Epstein indicated, "It is not possible for the mind of the thinking man to know everything. It is only the ignorant who feel that they know everything. . . . The great mind, the really intelligent mind, realizes that the limits of knowledge are entirely beyond its grasp." Next, the rabbi summarized his answer to the question about the basis of religious certainty posed in his thesis:

> Whatever is in man must be in the universe. Do we recognize honor? Then honor exists. Do we know love? Then love exists. Have we become inspired by a high sense of duty? Then duty exists. Such invisible realities come not from mere bones and sinew. They exist in the universe and are manifested by us. When we speak of that Power who possesses love, and justice, and truth, and mercy, and other untold . . . excellences, in the infinite degree, we speak of what we call God. Can we justly attack such a foundation for religion?[25]

The rabbi's obvious answer to his rhetorical inquiry was that we cannot. Epstein's manner of dealing with the seemingly contradictory was typically Aristotelian, although it also reflected his uncle's use of logic in Talmudic discourse. Individuals had to maintain a balance between "complete faith" and "complete self reliance." Harry Epstein spent a lifetime struggling with this juggling act.[26]

Still another element of Harry Epstein's world view was his concept of the family. As to be expected, the home was respected and supported in the rabbi's sermons. It formed a part of his organic view of society, and it served as an educational repository for the child. The following aphorisms were typical: "A child born into a home of ideals has inherited the finest and the best which life can give him." "The parent is the High Priest in the sanctuary of the home." "[The] Home [is the] beautiful School of [the] Jew. [It] made him soft and tender and developed [a] fine Jewish life." We previously noted that Epstein believed that Judaism had to be woven into daily activities for it to be meaningful. This process would logically occur within the home.[27]

Epstein's marriage confirmed his positive outlook. He married Reva Chashesman shortly after arriving in Atlanta. Reva was a brilliant young woman born into an equally Orthodox and prestigious rabbinic family in Russian Poland. Her father taught her at home from a very early age. By her fifth birthday she could read Hebrew, Yiddish, and German. Her mother, an educated linguist in her own right, offered to pay a local teacher to allow Reva into the classroom. She would be the first Jew and younger than the other children. Reva attended until an inspector visited the school and demanded her expulsion even after she had responded well to his many questions. During World War I, her town was largely destroyed, and the family was forced to live in a barn with another family.[28]

After the war Reva became the first Jewish girl to attend and then graduate (with honors) from the Suvalki gymnasium. She was offered a scholarship to a Polish university, which she refused because of the anti-Semitism she would have had to confront. A brother was studying medicine at the University of Berlin, where she joined him. She majored in literature and languages and minored in art. She pursued her studies in Europe after her parents relocated to Chicago. Desirous of learning French, she enrolled at the Sorbonne. Her parents finally convinced Reva to matriculate at the University of Chicago, where she graduated magna cum laude three weeks before her marriage. Reva Epstein was offered a fellowship and could have followed a career as a college language and literature instructor. Instead, she chose to use her abilities as the *rebbetzin*.

Reva Chashesman, the only Jewish gymnasium student in her school. Poland, ca. 1922. Reproduced by permission of Atlanta Jewish Heritage Center
and Rabbi and Mrs. Harry H. Epstein.

As the rabbi's wife she supported Hadassah actively, serving as its area and regional education commission chairperson. She conducted model Hebrew classes and study groups, and she helped the younger women of the congregation learn the customs and cooking traditions associated with the Jewish holidays. She was deeply involved with the Jewish National Fund, the Atlanta women's division having been established in her home in the early 1970s. She also was committed to the women's division of Israeli bonds and to the congregation sisterhood. When people speak of Reva Epstein, they tend to mention such qualities as wisdom, graciousness, charm, brilliance, understanding, and judgment. She is widely viewed within the congregation as the ideal *rebbetzin*.

More importantly for our understanding of Harry Epstein, Reva became perhaps his closest friend and confidante. They would share things together that he did not feel comfortable sharing with congregants. She lived the role of the ideal *rebettzin*, as their values and causes seemed to interact harmoniously. While Harry counseled the husband in a troubled marriage in the study, she served as the sounding board for the wife in the living room. Even more given to ceremony than her husband, Reva Epstein opposed him within the household in his efforts to affiliate the congregation with the Conservative movement. Unlike his father, who stopped writing letters and became cool after what he perceived as a betrayal, Reva and Reva's father (who had come to live with the Epsteins as a widowed rabbi emeritus) supported Harry Epstein personally and understood necessity.

The adjectives for describing Harry and Reva Epstein's relationship would include devoted, loving, supportive, and sacrificing. Their daughters, Davida and Renana, obtained college degrees from Brandeis and the University of Chicago. Having spent summers in Chicago with their grandparents, they both married Chicago men. Renana, in fact, married the son of a president of her grandfather Ephraim Epstein's congregation.

Harry Epstein's own warm family life was not necessarily a reflection of his childhood. Although he dedicated his book *Judaism and Progress* "To my parents: In gratitude for their sacrifices in my behalf," Epstein's youth and his relations with his father had not been as happy as they might have been. As previously indicated, Ephraim Epstein's persona laid claim to more respect than love. When Harry wrote "My Tribute to a Distinguished Father," on the

Rabbi Harry H. Epstein and his father, Rabbi Ephraim Epstein. Chicago, Ill., ca. 1940s. Reproduced by permission of Atlanta Jewish Heritage Center and Rabbi Harry H. Epstein.

latter's thirty-fifth anniversary in Chicago, the message was one of homage and resembled tributes he wrote for great men, rather than stemming from a close filial relationship. Ephraim Epstein had had an incalculable impact on his son, but the son was aware that all families were not ideal.

Actually, when one searches for references to the family in Harry Epstein's writings, the lack of such is as noteworthy as are the notations themselves. Frequently, too, the remarks were not complimentary. Epstein recognized that "all powerful forces [the family, modern science, the written word and religion amongst them, were] double-edged swords, [which] can be used for good or ill." He denounced parents for not creating a positive Jewish environment in the 1960s, and for being "derelicts in life" in the 1930s. Too many parents played cards and left their children in the hands of nurses with whom they personally would have had nothing to do.[29]

When placed in the context of his attitude toward other critical institutions, an analysis of Epstein's views concerning the family adds insight into his general conceptualization of institutions, ideas, and individuals. Although he recognized the necessity of government and took pride in the accomplishments of the United States, he was far from an uncritical jingoist. While he preached respect and devotion to religion and congregational life, he described their failures, trials, and tribulations as well. Harry Epstein believed that institutions could be used for benevolence, or could be subverted (they were "double-edged swords") by the individuals managing them. Thus, the key was the righteousness, honesty, and integrity of the people acting within the group. Unlike conservative clergy and political philosophers—with Montesquieu leading the list—who put their trust in institutions to curb individual behavior, Harry Epstein placed his faith behind the lifting up of the individual through a firm set of values to improve civilization. As he said, "Truth, Justice, Peace—[these were the] pillars upon which [an] ordered world depends." If one of these were to be "weakened or destroyed[, the] whole structure or civilization [would] topple over."[30]

It would be a mistake to treat or think of Harry Epstein's ideas and experiences as if he were a unique or isolated individual. As noted previously, Epstein shared much in common with Leo Jung and Joseph Lookstein. This commonality included images of religion and world view. In each instance, as they blended old and new, a synthesis was arrived at with scanty theological support. These men told their congregations of the importance of institutions, of being "Jewish," of the family, of community, and their place in American society. They viewed themselves and their interpretation as superior without really coming to terms with the compromises they were making. Like Epstein, it was not unusual for young men of his generation and background to reject careers in law and medicine because they perceived themselves as being pioneers in modern Orthodoxy, and as missionaries to retain the second generation within Judaism and, in fact, to keep Judaism alive. To appeal to this group, as the study of Rabbi Epstein's thoughts make clear, a family-centered middle class morality displaced deep theological discourse.

This philosophy of the middle class transcended intra-denominational boundaries and thus facilitated Epstein's move from modern Orthodox to Conservative ranks. Milton Steinberg, who may be viewed as the pulpit rabbi as intellectual, headed New York's Park Avenue Synagogue from the 1930s to his death in 1950. He defined the "central task" of the Conservative rabbi as the teaching of a "philosophy of life." He treated social problems in relation to Jewish tradition. A traditionalist who opposed assimilation and took pride in Jewish identity, he nonetheless supported modifications in ritual when they were "practical." As a student he, too, wrestled with the problem of reason and faith. The struggle continued throughout his career as he contrasted the Hebrews and Greeks. What emerged for Steinberg, like Epstein, was a "rational theology" that valued scientific inquiry ennobled with ethics, values, and faith. A close supporter of Mordecai Kaplan, Steinberg was too much of a theist to join the Reconstructionist camp outright. Yet, he shared the sense of folkways and peoplehood, a sense reflected in his cultural approach to Zionism.[31]

Serving congregations in Cleveland and Chicago, Solomon Goldman used the same methodology, rationale, and middle class philosophy as Steinberg, Epstein, and the moderate spokesmen of modern Orthodoxy. Preferring the term "traditional," Goldman stressed ethical and cultural continuity. Judaism had to be relevant, scientific, and alive, but faith and intuition filled the void when reason had reached its limits. All people were interdependent and equal, and individuals exercised free will. People should act righteously and seek a moral ideal. To Goldman, also, the synagogue and Zionism both served as agents of regeneration.

The "community of manners," as historian Jenna W. Joselit terms it, nurtured by these rabbinic leaders might be seen almost as an historical imperative. Perhaps for many individuals in various locales it was. Yet, individuals like Rabbi Geffen of Atlanta and Rabbi Heiman of Minneapolis do not appear to have traveled nearly as far along the spectrum of acculturation, and recent experiences in Atlanta and studies of successful Orthodox enclaves further underline the conclusion that perceived circumstances influence people's decisions, but that individuals also make choices. Harry Epstein developed a philosophy of life based on a foundation of Jewish peoplehood and culture through which his congregation could flourish, and with which he could feel satisfied that he was serving his mission well and satisfying his duty.

7

On Highs and Lows

Although Harry Epstein's worldview was highly consistent and appeared to be fully developed very early, it was not static. It reflected different periods in his life and career. From his earliest articles on the Hebron yeshiva well into the 1950s, the rabbi remained largely optimistic. Even while witnessing Hitler and the Israeli War for Independence, he saw hope for humanity and expected a transformation of values ushering in the flourishing of culture and the advancement of civilization. He was remarkably forgiving and understanding of human frailties to the point of counseling forbearance toward Germany. One can sense the exuberance the rabbi put into his speeches and writings, and the enthusiasm with which he organized and led various organizations. He spent considerable time forging liaisons with other Jews and with gentiles, in behalf of denominational dynamism and brotherhood, respectively. This period lasted from the time he was in his twenties through his mid fifties. He was ambitious personally and for his congregation, and he enjoyed facing challenges.

The trials and tribulations of being in the *galut,* or exile from Israel, were in the forefront of Epstein's thought. His theme during the 1920s was reaching out to the youth in America by mixing progress with tradition while opposing materialism. During the 1930s through the 1940s, emphasis shifted in reaction to changing circumstances. Now, the critical issue was fighting anti-Semitism as epitomized by Adolf Hitler. Expressing opposition to militarism, Epstein wanted to strike at this challenge on a moral plane until resort to force became unavoidable. A continuing preoccupation was the establishment of the state of Israel as a safety valve for European suffering, but also as a means of revitalizing Jewish culture. Epstein was much consumed with the concepts of democracy and evolutionary progress. During these years, he tended to see issues as dichotomous. Monotheism juxtaposed paganism. Idealism juxtaposed materialism. Modern Orthodoxy juxtaposed Reform. The maintenance of tradition stood in contrast with assimilation. The rabbi had a firm purpose and clear message. God would prevail over savagery.

As Atlanta's German Jewish Reform community and its Rabbi Marx had represented the Jews to the general community previously, Rabbi Epstein and his upwardly mobile, growing, and vibrant East European congregation came to assume this role and recognition during the 1930s. Whereas Marx fell into disrepute as the Holocaust and the creation of Israel made his anti-Zionism and his seemingly accommodationist position anachronistic, Epstein appeared to be on the top of issues and in the forefront of a dynamic traditionalism. After World War II, under Jacob Rothschild—even though he espoused Zionism—the Temple's mission continued to be narrowly circumscribed by the society. There would be liaison with the Christian community and, with the reluctant support of the congregation, service in the fostering of positive race relations. German Jewish leadership and power receded as Epstein guided his people onward and outward.

The quarter century beginning in 1950 witnessed the crowning glory of Harry Epstein's career. When Ahavath Achim voted to affiliate with the Conservative movement in 1952, it was cited as the largest such congregation in the South.[1] During these years Epstein achieved his greatest personal acclaim. He presided over the Rabbinical Assembly of the Southeastern states, served on several national boards, and guided the local and regional O.R.T. These were the years also in which he witnessed the building of the Harry H. Epstein/Solomon Schecter (Jewish day) School, and in which he led his congregation into a new building following the flow of the membership northward in the city and into the ranks as one of the two largest Conservative congregations in America. These were the years of the testimonial dinners in his honor, of the receipt of awards, of sabbaticals spent in Israel, of Israeli forests planted in his and Reva's names, and of a dormitory at the Jewish Theological Seminary dedicated to Reva. Epstein now supervised grandchildren of his original students through the bar and bat mitzvah ceremonies and continued to counsel against hatred, this time with reference to Israel's Six Day War.[2]

During the 1950s and 1960s, the world seemed more complicated and the issues more diverse. It was no longer a matter of actualizing the Zionist dream. Now, the nature of support, the relationship between American and Israeli Jews, and the character of an extant state of Israel were of import. Current issues facing Americans were discussed, but these issues appeared less dramatic and less associated with Jewishness. Epstein opposed the Cold War, communism, and McCarthyism, advocated peace in an atomic age, and supported civil rights for blacks and later for women. He related his stands to Jewish values, but the situations did not seem so pressing. There are not many speeches in his extensive archives on the Korean or the Vietnamese conflicts. The revolt of youth received understanding in its scant notice, but it only seemed to fulfill longterm prophecies. While emphasis, if there was any, was on American events, the rabbi also addressed the state of the synagogue, history, education, and, especially after the mid 1960s, the significance of family-related issues. Every year brought celebration of Israel's gains and anniversaries, and support for Atlanta Jewish Federation fund-raising. No longer did Rabbi Epstein refer to the trials of *galut*. It is clear that he was speaking to American Jews about their problems and responsibilities as Americans and as Jews without the negative connotations of diaspora.[3]

From the late 1960s until his retirement in 1982, Epstein returned to themes from his early ministry. He expressed concern for declining religiosity. He opposed apathy, intermarriage, and assimilation, and he again stressed the meaning of Judaism and its traditions for life. He also returned to a denunciation of materialism. Yet, the tone of Harry Epstein's message was frequently less optimistic than before. He became more resigned. He no longer expected great advances as he had as a man of twenty-five or thirty-five.

To the interviewer during the 1980s, the rabbi bemoaned the decision to join the Conservative ranks. Conservatism had become too nebulous. It lacked substance and was too willing to compromise fundamentals. Epstein perceived very little difference between Conservative and Reform, and he believed that many Conservative rabbis were virtually Deistic in their perception of God. Reason had fought with faith and won the day. The rabbi seemed to feel that his actions only delayed and may have even exacerbated an almost inevitable decline.

Harry Epstein told the story of the rabbi of Tzanz. As a young man this rabbi hoped to reform the world. When he grew older he concluded that this task was too tall an order for one man. He would reform one country. Later, the rabbi of Tzanz became contented with the goal of perfecting his community, and then simply his family. Finally, the rabbi accepted the responsibility of perfecting himself as "a sufficiently demanding task." Did not Rabbi Epstein associate himself with the life cycle of the rabbi of Tzanz?

During the last fifteen years, Rabbi Epstein had the aid of assistant rabbis. This aid involved supervision and the inevitable conflicts over roles and personalities, but it also meant that Epstein was partly relieved of some of his responsibilities. He may have been relying on previous sermon materials more, or simply on his years of experience. Yet, sermon notes indicate that the rabbi was not preparing either as systematically or as energetically as was the case previously. There are fewer quotations and less reliance on history and comparative religion. Issues were viewed as more gray than black and white. Congregants continued to refer to his brilliance as a speaker, but some who wish to remain anonymous suggest that active participation and observance declined. A cult of personality had arisen around Rabbi Epstein, which seemed to supplant loyalty and support of the congregation per se. As was natural in a congregation with more than two thousand families, it became difficult for him to familiarize himself with new members, especially if they were not descendants of longtime families.

More surprisingly, Harry Epstein lost touch with what became the leading organizations of the Atlanta Jewish community. After his conflict with Ed Kahn, he did not develop relations with the next two executive directors of the Atlanta Jewish Federation, or with their staffs. This break was not necessarily Epstein's doing. It reflected a change of power within Atlanta paralleling similar developments in Jewish communities throughout the country. Authority was shifting from ministerial to lay hands and to the hands of the professional managers of fund-raising and social service agencies, and from the congregation to the federation and community center. To Epstein it appeared that the federation had usurped the function of speaking for all things Jewish. It had become an overly scientific machine that had lost the human touch. The federation "needs a sense of values"—that idealism which was so crucial to the rabbi. The rabbi was consigned to his role within the congregation and to citywide rabbinic organizations, or arms of lay-governed national bodies.

The Atlanta Jewish population had multiplied from perhaps eleven or twelve thousand when the rabbi first arrived in the city to an estimated fifty-nine thousand by 1985. Although the number of congregations increased from five to sixteen between 1968 and 1988, almost two-thirds of Atlanta's Jewish families were unaffiliated with congregations. The situation no longer prevailed in which a few rabbis acted as the spokesmen, or even critical leaders, for the Jewish community at large. Thus, institutional and demographic trends reinforced the tendencies of changes in career and life stages.[4]

Harry Epstein had heard rumors of grumblings within the congregation. In 1978 a correspondence was begun concerning his and the congregation's future. Many still wanted Epstein as their rabbi, but others sought change. Some leaders started to communicate with the rabbi about a friendly, gradual transition. Almost inevitably, feathers were ruffled. Epstein was replaced by Arnold Goodman, the president of the national Rabbinical Assembly at the time of his selection.[5]

It was natural for the new rabbi to make alterations in establishing his authority, style, and ceremonial practices, which the old rabbi would frown on as counter to tradition. Conscious that his father's congregation cut off support for his mother a few years after his father's death, Epstein made certain that provisions for himself and his wife were specified in contractual form, delineating the manner in which they would continue to participate in the life of the congregation in a respected fashion.

In a very real sense, Rabbi and Mrs. Epstein thought of the congregants and Ahavath Achim as their family, and of the congregation almost as their child. As it matured, they desired the familial relationship to continue without any ill will. Epstein was honored in his receipt of emeritus status, with the sanctuary dedicated to him and his wife, and in other ways as well. Harry Epstein remained extremely active. He continued to conduct life cycle events—especially weddings and funerals for longtime members—to counsel and to give speeches. He finally had more time to spend with family and with the interested historian.

Rabbi and Mrs. Harry H. Epstein upon the occasion of the Achavath Achim sanctuary-naming in their honor. Atlanta, Ga., December 1982. Reproduced by permission of Atlanta Jewish Heritage Center and Rabbi and Mrs. Harry H. Epstein.

8

Denouement

Although ultimately he was the perennial optimist, Harry Epstein's relative sense of despair and his disillusionment with Conservatism may be taken as symptomatic of questions about religion with which he had grappled for much of his life. He asked Rabbi Sher in Slobodka more than sixty years ago if it was possible to teach people the fundamentals of Judaism: to love God and one's fellow human beings; and the basis of all religion: the balance between faith and reason. While striving to answer these questions, Rabbi Epstein lived a Judaism of compromise and adjustment. Was it possible to delineate the boundaries of accommodation? Once one accepted rabbinical authority for each generation to interpret the scriptures, laws, and ceremonies, was there an authoritative answer to any question?

Epstein's Orthodox family background and personal practices conflicted with a perception of the state of American Jews and Judaism. This perception was mediated by a very rational approach to the study of the Talmud and a desire to apply and adapt Judaism to the modern, voluntaristic American landscape. The solution he offered was a mixture of faith and reason, traditionalism and modernism—a mixture that he helped define as Conservative Judaism. He sought the benefits of both worlds. Had he been allowed to pursue a career in medicine and science, a direction his father's power over him precluded, he might have solved his personal dilemma by entering wholeheartedly into the realm of reason. Had he done so, however, his congregants and those he touched would not have gained the manifold benefits of his counsel and the insights of his long quest for understanding the fundamental ordered relationships of life.

In a broader historical context, one might conjecture that the German Jewish experience of the nineteenth century was one of Napoleonic emancipation and enlightened rationalism. These forces were briefly interrupted during the last gasps of mid-century monarchism, only to be resumed with the boundless opportunities and relative lack of prejudice in the United States. The East European experience was harsher. Life in late-nineteenth-century Russia involved not merely discriminatory laws, but also murder at the hands of the government-instigated mobs of the pogrom. Escape to American freedom was tempered during the twentieth century with the almost constant knowledge of and association with events in Europe. From the Balkan Wars through World War I and the Holocaust, and then to the nearly constant attacks on Israel, the message American Jews read was that people were neither totally rational nor loving. In America the German Jews of the last century chose the rationalism of Reform. East European Jews, including Harry Epstein, took the middle ground of Conservatism. The descendants of these individuals in the last quarters of the twentieth century elected to run the gamut in their responses from secularism, intermarriage, and assimilation, on the one hand, to neo-Orthodoxy and association with the Chabad Lubavitcher, a Hassidic group, on the other. Rabbi Epstein's life and ideas reflect the changing sands of time and the movement of feeling and thought. He served others by acting as a conduit for change.

Overview and Conclusion

During the seventeenth and eighteenth centuries in America, the pattern for congregational spiritual leadership followed the mode of Sephardic Jewry as it had been set in the Iberian Peninsula. The Spanish and Portuguese Jewish communities had risen socially, economically, politically, and intellectually under the rule of the Moors. Theirs was a worship of decorum and reason. The communities produced learned laymen like Maimonides, who adjudicated local disputes. Initially serving without salary, since one was not supposed to reap financial rewards from the study of the Torah, a few individuals gradually assumed a quasi-official status as community leaders starting in the fourteenth century. A division of function ensued, with separate roles for scholar, judge, teacher, and leader of ritual. In the Sephardic congregations the *parnas,* or president, and the *adjunta,* or board of trustees, held power over the *hazan,* or reader/cantor, who would lead the service, might perform some ritual functions, and might teach the youth.[1]

The Golden Age of Sephardic Jewry was followed by the Catholic Inquisition, driving Jews into exile or into secret worship as Marranos to avoid torture and death. Many of those who fled found homes in France, England, and Holland. Their practices were reinforced in Amsterdam, London, and the Caribbean colonies—which became virtual centers for colonial American Jewry—all of which accepted the Sephardic ritual, customs, and even language.

In the congregations founded in New York, Newport, Savannah, Charleston, and later Richmond and Philadelphia, when available, the unordained and usually only nominally educated *hazan* served as a poorly paid and powerless religious functionary. He would lead prayers and might obtain additional support through tutoring, performing Brith Milah (circumcision), or becoming a *shochet* (kosher butcher). Questions of *halakah,* or Jewish law, were answered by learned laymen, or referred to authorities in Europe. Offering mes-

114

sages to the congregation from the *parnas* and *adjunta,* the *hazan* might give two sermons per year.[2]

Gradually, as represented by the career of Gershom Mendes Seixas, the status of the position and its functions expanded. Asked to lead prayers for various causes by the government officials, called on as a representative for the Jewish community, and viewed as the equivalent of the more highly regarded Protestant clergy, the position of *hazan* rose in the perception of some congregations. Upwardly mobile Jews saw the need for a religious leader who could impress gentile opinion. With the increased prestige came a modicum of independence.

The nineteenth century witnessed what one historian has called the "Americanization of the synagogue" and what another has called the "Protestantization" of the rabbinate. These trends were actually interacting aspects of accommodation, reinforced by growing numbers of immigrants from German and Polish territory who succeeded in dominating congregational life. As congregations struggled with traditional and reform modes, with first one faction and then another holding sway, the position of *hazan*/rabbi became somewhat precarious, as illustrated by the protracted and conflict-ridden career of Abraham Rice, the first ordained rabbi to serve in America, and, during the 1850s by the firing from their jobs of every significant religious leader in the American pulpit.[3]

Nonetheless, success was possible if the individual was willing to adjust as the environment changed and if he had the appropriate background. The third ordained rabbi to travel to America, Max Lilienthal also had university training. He had been the leader of a government-sponsored Jewish educational system in Russia, from which he resigned when he realized that the underlying purpose was assimilation. After this failure, and his failure in New York trying to serve as chief rabbi of three congregations and as head of a *beth din,* or rabbinic court, he still retained the status to become spiritual leader of Cincinnati's B'nai Israel. Called by upper class German Jews striving for prestige, he was able to secure life tenure and a respectable salary. He served for twenty-seven years as an advocate of moderate Reform.[4]

Changes in central Europe paralleled what was about to occur in the United States. Jews had been granted limited citizenship and certain rights in France in 1791. The reforms were introduced in

other countries as Napoleon's armies spread through Europe. With
freedom it was hoped that Jews would assimilate. European secular
authorities attempted to undermine the role of the rabbi as they
undertook the assimilation of the Jews. No longer did the Jewish
communities—or their rabbis—have authority over civil law as they
had previously. Judicial functions were thus assumed by the state.
Marriage and ritual power was taken from the hands of the individual rabbi and granted to a *beth din*. Government licensure and secular
learning were required for admittance to the rabbinate in certain
countries. As secular education was made available to Jews, rabbinic
teaching responsibilities also declined in importance. Rabbis frequently followed itinerant careers, as their actions were dominated
by wealthy laymen.[5]

In Germany and, to a lesser extent in other parts of Europe, a small
band of individuals decided to make themselves more marketable. In
line with the Jewish enlightenment, or *Haskalah,* and to fulfill legal
requirements, they obtained university educations to complement
their religious studies and became "doctor-rabbis." Secular education
enabled them to communicate with their educated congregants and
to serve as spokesmen to the gentile community. They interacted
with their Christian counterparts, emulated their example, and
gained from their prestige. Their minds and hearts opened to modernity, if not various degrees of reform. They organized seminaries
and met in conferences. As the revolutions of 1848 crumbled, and
as new opportunities opened in America, some of these men came
to America, bringing with them the age of rabbinic giants and fo-
menting reform.

The handful of men who filled the pulpits of American congregations during the middle decades of the eighteen hundreds were
hardy, dynamic, and creative. In most cases lacking formal training
and ordination, they transformed the very structure of American
Jewry and the role of the rabbinate, virtually by the force of their
characters and through their visions. Perhaps the three most-important individuals were Isaac Leeser, Isaac Mayer Wise, and David
Einhorn. The last was an outspoken critic of slavery and an advocate
for radical Reform. Einhorn's was an independent voice presaging
the free pulpit of the twentieth century exemplified by Stephen S.
Wise. Leeser and Wise, one the traditionalist and the other the Re-
former, illustrate the role of rabbi as institution builder and national
leader. They (like Einhorn) provided educational materials and

prayer books. They edited newspapers to express their points of view and to bring the American Jewish community together. Both advocated and initiated publishing ventures, seminaries, and national meetings and organizations of rabbis and synagogue representatives. They traveled widely, and numerous congregations sprang up in their paths. Although all three were strong expositors of principle, Leeser and Wise probably provided more enduring service by attempting to moderate differences and bridge gaps. The three participated in Jewish and communal social service agency development, gave sermons in the vernacular (although for Einhorn this language was German), supervised and defined ritual practice, became spokesmen to the general community, and otherwise acted as the key religious leaders of various Jewish communities. Nevertheless, since they lacked substantive training and the civil government provided the court system, their scholarly and judicial roles atrophied.[6]

Einhorn and especially Leeser and Wise prepared the framework for the late-nineteenth and early-twentieth-century rabbis. They became public figures and national leaders whose examples were institutionalized. They had contributed to a sense of professionalism, if not oneness, among their rabbinical colleagues. Some of those who succeeded them were students of Wise's or of close colleagues, whereas others had undergone similar training in Germany. Such men as Bernard Felsenthal, Marcus Jastrow, Benjamin Szold, Sabato Morais, Henry Pereira Mendes, and Bernard Drachman solidifed their positions within congregations. Serving as theoreticians, these rabbis delineated the beliefs and practices of Reform and, in response, Orthodoxy and, later still, Conservativism and modern Orthodoxy. With the partition of Judaism into various branches, they established competing rabbinical and congregational organizations and seminaries.[7]

This was a dramatic era in Judaism, and change was perhaps the greatest constant. The transformation in the importance of the sermon and the implication of this change is a case in point. Many strands intertwine in its development. The sermon had become more significant in Germany, as rabbis became spokesmen for the Jewish community. Within America rabbis were influenced by Protestant and especially Episcopal clergy (from whom they even borrowed styles of apparel) and the popular chautauqua lecturers. Reform's Pittsburgh Platform of 1885 stressed the primacy of civic improvement and social conscience over ritual, in this way paralleling the ideas of the Protestant Social Gospel movement—a movement that influenced many rabbis in many affluent and acculturating congregations. The sermon became a tool not only for educating an adult population lacking a strong background in Jewish laws, history, and customs, but also for calling them into action in behalf of social causes espoused by their ministers. Such rabbis as David Marx thus emerged as social activists. As activists they worked with their Protestant colleagues and community builders and cemented their roles as spokesmen and exemplars of Jewish ideals to the gentile community. Building secular structures, these rabbis also came into the forefront when rationalizing Jewish community social service agencies. Somewhat specialized at first, these agencies broadened, confederated, and then federated for entire communities, as new waves of East European Jews flowed into America. What Jonathan Sarna has characterized as "the professionalization of the rabbinate" was well under way. Rabbis received specialized training, accepted recognized rules of conduct and even of dress, traveled widely giving speeches and attending conferences, and negotiated salaries and fringe benefits.[8]

As the roles and prestige of the rabbis increased dramatically, and as many rabbis started careers that often spanned three and more decades with the same congregations, a cult of personality developed. The synagogue, the Jewish community, and even worship and spirituality were intermingled with the character and personality of the individual rabbi. Another factor in this development may have been the increasing secularization of the congregants and the growing numbers who did not affiliate with a congregation at all. Coincidentally, the development of personality cults was a dimension reflected also in the Hassidic communities that were transplanted to America from the Holocaust.[9]

The last quarter of the nineteenth century brought pogroms, but also substantial ferment in Russia. A secularizing middle class was rising, as Jews were allowed to enter into a restricted urban life. This constituency and some of its rabbis were influenced by the *Maskil,* or East European version of the *Haskalah.* For a different class the labor union activities of the Bund and socialism weakened allegiance to the old rabbinic world. To a lesser degree as well, Zionism and the rise of Yiddish culture played their parts in this constriction of the role of the rabbi. Some rabbinical students traveled to western Poland and Germany in pursuance of their studies, while others remained in such areas as Lithuania. Even in the latter, as has been indicated, rabbinic training was noteworthy for experimentation.[10]

The East European immigrants in America who formed congregations typically hired rabbis steeped in the rabbi-as-scholar/judge tradition. They were accustomed to chief rabbis of the community who supervised various ritual activities, including *kashruth*. Yet, when communities called on such individuals as Jacob Joseph or Jacob David Willovsky to act as chief rabbi, or when they tried to centralize functions in the form of the old world *kehillah* (community), the attempts usually met with failure. Lacking civil sanction, and with dwindling community support, the East European Orthodox transplants were given to arguments among themselves, as they competed for prestige, authority, fees, and constituents. Like Tobias Geffen, many either lived in America while their thoughts and actions remained in Europe, or, like Ephraim Epstein, they grappled with attempts at minimal compromise to maintain their congregants' observance. Nonetheless, these rabbis had come voluntarily and were therefore somewhat more likely to acculturate, or at least mediate between their members and the challenges posed by American freedom. The later refugees of the 1930s and 1940s from Hitler and the Holocaust came involuntarily. Their rabbis, including Aaron Kotler, were far less willing to adjust.[11]

As the duties of the American rabbinate multiplied, certain functions were relegated to secondary importance, or delegated to specialists. Whereas, in the early history of the seminaries, pulpit rabbis performed as part-time teachers, scholarship and teaching became the purview of specialists, certainly by the 1920s. Few twentieth-century rabbis could emulate the examples of such pulpit scholars as Solomon Goldman, Hyman G. Enelow, Milton Steinberg, or Robert Gordis. It was the unusual individual, such as Mordecai Kaplan and Joseph Soloveitchek, who could mix his or her functions as educator and school administrator with those of denominational theoretician and, even more atypically, pulpit rabbi. Solomon Schecter of the Jewish Theological Seminary and Yeshiva University's Bernard Revel came to epitomize the rabbi as college president. Similar patterns developed vis-à-vis Jewish communal activities. By the 1930s, Jewish education, social service agencies, defense organizations, fund-raising and—by the 1950s—even the administration of national rabbinical associations were run more and more by specialists in those areas. The rabbi would serve on boards, ask for funds from congregants, supervise religious school principals, encourage Jewish day schools, and act as chairpeople of federation campaigns, but the impetus in these affairs came from elsewhere.[12]

The circumscription also was visible in the role of the rabbi as Jewish community spokesperson. The function emerging during the second quarter of the nineteenth century—and reaching its apex with the Reform rabbis of the 1890s and early 1900s—was assumed by community relations councils during the 1930s and 1940s, by federations, and by such specialized agencies as the American Jewish Congress, the American Jewish Committee, the Anti-Defamation League of B'nai B'rith, and even lay and rabbinic organizations. Leaders of these organizations, including the late Marc C. Tanenbaum, may be rabbis by training, but their role as spokespeople is predicated fundamentally on the basis of their expertise, organizational mission, and association.

The shift in role remains true even on the local level, where the functions of the synagogue and its spiritual leaders have been equally subsumed by diversity and specialization. Ironically, Mordecai Kaplan, Joseph Lookstein, and others who had pioneered in the synagogue-as-Jewish-community-center ideal, in the creation of bureaus of Jewish education, in federations of Jewish charity, and in other similar endeavors had sown the seeds of their own compartmentalization. The role of the rabbi as Jewish community leader had contracted by the 1950s. The rabbi became first and foremost the servant of the local congregation and, secondarily, a participant in local, national, and international organizations. He would prod his congregation, but he frequently found it difficult to lead because less was expected, or granted to him in the way of authority and prestige.[13]

Denominational differences partly determined the "outside" interests of rabbis. Many Orthodox and most Conservative rabbis were deeply involved in Zionism, while, prior to the late 1930s, Abba Hillel Silver and Max Heller were the exceptional Reform advocates of the state of Israel. Most were involved with overseas relief, but Orthodox rabbis tended to stress individual aid, especially to Yeshiva students and teachers. Reform rabbis usually were in the forefront of institutionalizing the granting of assistance and rationalizing fundraising efforts on a broader basis. Reform rabbis outside the South were more likely to be found in the forefront of the civil rights movement during the mid twentieth century. However, again, there were notable exceptions, such as Abraham Joshua Heschel. Orthodox and, to a lesser but growing extent, Conservative rabbis were more likely concerned with *kashruth* purity and the establishment and supervision of the *mikveh* or ritual bath. All have served as chaplains for penitentiaries and military installations, as Hillel directors, as opponents of anti-Semitism, and as spokesmen for Jewish-American patriotism.

Today, those who enter the rabbinate are confronted with many choices. Will they become pulpit rabbis and be expected to serve as not overly energetic oracles of social consciousness and religious observance, as fund-raisers, builders, administrators, counselors and pastors, pulpit orators, educational consultants and *b'nai mitzvot* tutors, board members for Jewish and secular associations, participants in local and national ministerial and rabbinic associations, and arbiters and leaders of ritual observance, et cetera et cetera? Will they pursue careers as social workers, educators, or administrators within Jewish organizations? With the Protestantization of the American Jewish clergy, it is assumed that they have a "calling." They also had better be professionals with broad educations and backgrounds who can deal with congregations in contract negotiations.[14]

Thus far, most of the rabbinic attributes dealt with can be viewed partly as job description-type categories. There are other characteristics less quantifiable. These characteristics include the rabbi as "symbolic exemplar." Under this category the rabbi is assumed to be morally superior to his congregation and to serve as a symbol of living Judaism. He is supposed to live morally even if his congregants do not. He is expected to observe the *halakah*, or law, diligently even if his congregants do not. This role harks back to the old rabbi-as-sage/moral-leader ideal, but with the difference that during the late Middle Ages distinctions between congregants and rabbi were more of degree than quality. Thus today, congregants have a tendency to view the rabbi as their surrogate in these areas. As in so many instances, the historian's observations must be open to exceptions and modification. During the last few decades, with the rise of ethnic pride and identity has come a flourish of ritual observance and life practice among practitioners of each branch of Judaism. Thus, declining participation of some is counterposed with increased activity of others. Finally, rabbis, by the very nature of their duties and their inclinations, also have served as cultural brokers. In this fashion they have attempted to mediate in the process of adaptation to American life. Their counsel and actions run the spectrum from the maintenance of absolute tradition through various degrees of accommodation to total assimilation.[15]

Where, then, can we place Rabbi Harry H. Epstein? As is to be expected when dealing with a particular individual, and especially one whose career spanned five decades, Epstein does not fit into any single category. He participated in various transitional roles in terms of job description. For the first generation congregants, he provided the role of scholar/sage through his Talmudic knowledge and the discussion groups he led and through his utilization of Yiddish. He helped to communicate to them also the needs of the next generation. To the acculturating immigrant and the second generation, he brought his secular knowledge, the use of learned English sermons, decorum, and other changes in the service, including mixed seating, a structured educational system for children as well as adults, and a series of clubs and communication devices to retain Jewish identity and at least a modicum of learning and ritual. Thus, he served as a catalyst for both change and continuity, as he eased his congregants into the Conservative mold. He offered arbitration as a judge in the old world sense and gave counsel and succor as expected of a modern American rabbi/pastor. He helped develop local social service agencies and served as a spokesperson and symbol of the Jews to non-Jews in a manner comparable to that of German American rabbis when their subcommunities underwent a similar period of adjustment. In this and other ways, he assisted his congregants in their desire to be accepted and to succeed in the secular world. Yet, his role as spokesperson and as nurturer of social service functions was limited, as these areas became the domain of trained professional specialists and affluent lay people, who felt more comfortable dealing directly with the Christian community and making the critical financial decisions. He worked in behalf of first Orthodox and then Conservative rabbinic and congregational bodies and involved his congregants, as another method for them to remain Jewish and express themselves in Jewish causes in ways that would reflect their rising status in business. He actively opposed anti-Semitism, supported the needs of Jews overseas, and championed Zionism. Again, one observes continuity with his roots and with East European traditions, intermingled with new methods and perceptions. Harry Epstein built the towering figure of the rabbi based on the East

European model, as magnified by mid-twentieth-century American wants and expectations. He worked in the field long enough to witness the power and majesty of the rabbi decline, as the needs of his divergent constituents were radically transformed and their relationship to the congregation and numerous other groups underwent fundamental metamorphosis. Thus, the saga of Rabbi Harry Epstein is the story of a man, of a profession, and of a generation responding to change.

Notes

Introduction

1. On the different movements within American Judaism, see Marc Lee Raphael, *Profiles in American Judaism: The Reform, Conservative, Orthodox and Reconstructionist Traditions in Historical Perspective* (San Francisco: Harper and Row, 1984), and Jonathan Sarna, ed., "The American Rabbinate: A Centennial View," *American Jewish Archives* (November 1983). Raphael questions the nineteenth-century "Orthodoxy" of American Jewry as well as the late-nineteenth-century antecedents of Conservatism. For "resisters versus accommodators," see Jeffrey S. Gurock," Resisters and Accommodators: Varieties of Orthodox Rabbis in America, 1886–1983," in Sarna, ed., "The American Rabbinate," 100–187. Gurock emphasizes the variety of responses, as does Jonathan Sarna, "The Spectrum of Jewish Leadership in Ante-Bellum America," *Journal of American Ethnic History* (Spring 1982): 59–67, and John Higham, ed., *Ethnic Leadership in America* (Baltimore: Johns Hopkins University Press, 1978). Although Gurock's terms "resisters" and "accommodators" are used here, Christopher J. Kauffman defines similar Catholic respondents as "transformationists" and "preservationists" in *Tradition and Transformation in Catholic Culture* (New York: Macmillan, 1987).

2. Marshall Sklare, *Conservative Judaism: An American Religious Movement* (New York: Free Press, 1955); Moshe Davis, *The Emergence of Conservative Judaism: The Historical School in Nineteenth Century America* (Philadelphia: Jewish Publication Society, 1963); and sources in n. 1 above. Lance J. Sussman describes as "problematic" whether Isaac Leeser, and by implication nineteenth-century traditional Judaism, was a forerunner of contemporary Conservatism or Orthodoxy. This concept balances the conflict between Sklare and Davis concerning the origins of Conservative Judaism. Sussman, "The Life and Career of Isaac Leeser (1806–1868): A Study of American Judaism in Its Formative Period" (Ph.D. diss., Hebrew Union College—Jewish Institute of Religion, 1987), 414. Michael R. Weisser describes a group of individuals from the rural areas of the shtetls who never found much success within New York and attempted to retain the traditional world view in *A Brotherhood of Memory: Jewish Landsmanshaftn in the New World* (New York: Basic Books, 1985). See especially Jeffrey S. Gurock, "A Stage in the Emergence of the Americanized Synagogue among East European Jews: 1890–1910," *Journal of American Ethnic History* (Spring 1990): 7–25.

Chapter 1. Lithuanian Roots

1. Actually, Harry Epstein indicates that the family name was originally Bakst. It was changed by his great-grandfather to avoid military service. According to Rabbi Epstein, as religious functionaries members of the Levi tribe were excused, and the name Epstein was associated with membership in that group. Harry H.

Epstein interview by this author, June–July 1986 (hereafter cited as Epstein/Bauman interview). On life and culture in the shtetl, see Mark Zborowski and Elizabeth Herzog, *Life is with People: The Culture of the Shtetl* (New York: Schocken, 1952); Solomon Simon, *In the Thicket* (Philadelphia: Jewish Publication Society, 1963); A. S. Sachs, *Worlds That Passed* (Philadelphia: Jewish Publication Society, 1928); Alfred Erich Senn, *The Emergence of Modern Lithuania* (New York: Columbia University Press, 1958); Diane and David Roskies, *The Shtetl Book* (New York: KTAV, 1979); Steven Zipperstein, *The Jews of Odessa: A Cultural History, 1794–1881* (Stanford, Calif.: Stanford University Press, 1986); and Weisser, *Brotherhood of Memory.* Hyman L. Meites incorrectly claims that Ephraim Epstein was born in Swenchani, Russia, in Meites, ed., *History of The Jews of Chicago* (Chicago: Jewish Historical Society of Illinois, 1924), 487.

2. On this and following, see sources cited in introduction, n.2 (previous page) above and "Pale of Settlement," *Encyclopaedia Judaica,* vol. 13 (Jerusalem: Macmillan, 1972), 24–28; Zosa Szajkowski, "How the Mass Migration to America Began," *Jewish Social Studies* (October 1942), 291–310.

3. On this and following, Epstein/Bauman interview; Arcadius Kahan, *Essays in Jewish Social and Economic History,* ed. Roger Weiss (Chicago and London: University of Chicago Press, 1986), especially p. 48 for 1897 census figures table; "Lithuania," *Encyclopaedia Judaica,* vol. 11, 365–80; William B. Helmreich, *The World of the Yeshiva: An Intimate Portrait of Orthodox Judaism* (New York: Free Press, 1982), chap. 1; Raphael Mahler, *Hasidism and the Jewish Enlightenment: Their Confrontation in Galicia and Poland in the First Half of the Nineteenth Century* (Philadelphia: Jewish Publication Society, 1985); Hillel Goldberg, *Israel Salanter: Text, Structure, Idea* (New York: KTAV, 1982); idem., *Between Berlin and Slobodka* (Hoboken, N.J.: KTAV, 1989); Louis Ginzberg, *Students, Scholars and Saints* (Philadelphia: Jewish Publication Society, 1928); J. J. Weinberg, "The Musar Movement and Lithuanian Jewry," in Leo Jung, ed., *Men of the Spirit* (New York: Kymson, 1964), 215–83; Jonathan Frankel, *Prophecy and Politics: Socialism, Nationalism and the Russian Jew, 1862–1917* (New York: Cambridge University Press, 1981); Henry J. Tobias, *The Jewish Bund in Russia: From Its Origins to 1905* (Stanford, Calif.: Stanford University Press, 1972); Ezra Mendelsohn, *Class Struggle in the Pale* (Cambridge: Cambridge University Press, 1970); Raphael Abramovitch, "The Jewish Socialist Movement in Russia and Poland (1897–1919)," in *The Russian People: Past and Present,* vol. 2 (New York: Central Yiddish Culture Organization, 1948), 369–98. Harry Epstein's Hebrew name is Zvi Chaim.

4. On this and following, see Epstein/Bauman interview; "Epstein, Moses [*sic!*] Mordecai," *Encyclopaedia Judaica,* vol. 6, 835–36; "Slobodka Yeshiva," Ibid., vol. 14, 1668–69; "Kaunas," Ibid., vol. 10, 846–50; Zalman F. Ury, "Salanter's Musar Movement," in Leon D. Stitskin, ed., *Studies in Judaica* (New York: KTAV, 1972), 221–85; Charles S. Liebman, "The Training of American Rabbis," *American Jewish Yearbook 1968,* vol. 69, ed. Morris Fine and Milton Himmelfarb (New York: American Jewish Committee, 1968), 5–11; Hillel Goldberg, "Israel Salanter's Suspended Conversation," *Tradition* 22 (Fall 1986), 31–43. In n.9, p. 43, Goldberg indicates that "Slobodka generated the most intellectual offshoots usually at the highest level." Ephraim Shimoff, *Rabbi Isaac Elchanan Spektor* (New York: Yeshiva University Press, 1959), and especially the excellent series of sketches by Aaron Rakeffet-Rothkoff in *Jewish Life,* including "The 'Meitsheter Illui'" (November–December 1967), 29–35; "The Telsher Rav and Rosh Hayeshivah" (September–October 1968), 47–52; "The Last Rabbi of Kovno" (March–April 1968), 35–40; "The Kaminetzer Rosh Yeshivah: Rabbi Boruch Ber Leibowitz" (July–August 1969), 41–46; "The Mirrer Rosh Yeshivah" (May–June 1969), 41–47; "Reb Yitzchak Blaser: A Mussar

Giant" (Spring 1976), 43–48. In these articles, Rakeffet-Rothkoff describes key individuals, the teaching methods and ideas, and dislocations. On Musar and its significance for American Orthodoxy, see Jacob B. Angus, "The Orthodox Stream," *Guideposts in Modern Judaism* (New York: Bloch, 1954), reprinted in Jacob Neusner, ed., *Understanding American Judaism: Toward the Description of a Modern Judaism II* (New York: KTAV, 1975), 107–15. The breakup over teaching emphasis did not result in personal animus. Ephraim Epstein asked, and Rabbi Leibowitz consented, to be one of the officiating rabbis at Harry Epstein's wedding while Leibowitz visited Chicago. Interview with Rabbi Harry H. Epstein conducted by this author, 15 November 1989.

5. Epstein/Bauman interview; *Southern Israelite,* 3 September 1982. In this retirement interview Epstein called his father the greatest influence on his life. See also Rakeffet-Rothkoff articles cited in n.4 above.

6. On this and following, see Epstein/Bayman interview; Meites, *Chicago,* 487; Sara J. Geffen, "The Academies of Kovno and Slobodka," in Joel Ziff, ed., *Lev Tuviah* (privately published, 1988); Harry Epstein's response to synagogue dedication, 11 December 1982, "Ahavath Achim Synagogue Dedication, 1982–83," Harry H. Epstein Collection, Jewish Community Archives of the Jewish Heritage Center, Atlanta Jewish Federation. All other Epstein manuscripts and scrapbooks are from this collection if not otherwise noted. Since the papers were used during the initial processing stage, folder names should be viewed as descriptive and may not reflect the final titles.

7. Raphael, *Profiles,* 223, n.6; Meites, *Chicago,* 144, 486–88, 231, 234, 290–94, 324, 336–39, 348, 631, 652, 762; Epstein/Bauman interview. Ephraim Epstein was always an active member of the organizations to which he belonged. When he attended the eleventh convention of the Order Knights of Zion in 1908, for example, he served on the procedures and nominations committee. He was one of four speakers to address the American Jewish Relief Committee in 1914. He also served on the national advisory board of Mizrachi. Zosa Szajkowski, "Private and Organized American Jewish Overseas Relief (1914–1918)," *American Jewish Historical Quarterly* (September 1967): 52–136; Aaron Rakeffet-Rothkoff, *The Silver Era in American Jewish Orthodoxy: Rabbi Eliezer Silver and His Generation* (New York: Yeshiva University Press, 1981), 325.

A longtime friend and colleague and former president of the Hebrew Theological College described Ephraim Epstein as "ethical, humane, kind and helpful." With an aristocratic bearing, he was a leader who provided a model of selfless energy and personally raised "huge" amounts of money for refugee aid and education. He was respected by all elements of the community. Telephone interview of Leonard Mishkin by this author, 24 November 1986.

Chicago was in the forefront in the movement to assist refugees during the era of the First World War. Epstein joined with other Chicagoans to establish the Palestine Fund Committee in 1914. The Bread for Palestine and the Zionist Provisional Fund followed. These efforts led to the creation of the American Jewish Relief Committee, even though the latter was instigated by the New York–centered American Jewish Committee, and finally the Joint Distribution Committee. Joseph C. Hyman, *Twenty-five Years of American Aid to Jews Overseas* (Philadelphia: Jewish Publication Society, 1939); Oscar Handin, *A Continuing Task: The American Jewish Joint Distribution Committee, 1914–1964* (New York: Random House, 1964).

8. Joseph Friederman, "A Concise History of Agudah Israel," in *Yaacov Rosenheim Memorial Volume* (New York: 1963); "Orthodoxy," *Encyclopaedia Judaica,* vol. 12, 1488; Epstein/Bauman interview; Saul Abelson, "Chicago's Hebrew Theological College," Union of Orthodox Congregations of America *1947 Yearbook,* 160–68;

Leonard C. Mishkin, "History of the Hebrew Theological College/Bet Hamidrash LaTorah," Hebrew Theological College Sixtieth Anniversary *Journal,* 1982; Mishkin, "The Rabbi Ephraim Epstein Story," 4 October 1956, Eightieth Birthday Celebration Program; Harold P. Smith, "Hebrew Theological College: Its Impact on Chicago and World Jewry," Hebrew Theological College *Journal,* 1980; *New York Times,* 15 July 1960; *Chicago Sun-Times,* 15 July 1960; *Chicago Herald-American,* 13 December 1943; "Chicago, Illinois" folder; *Southern Israelite,* 19 September 1936; Epstein scrapbooks; Kollel Program, "Ephraim Epstein" folder; Meites, *Chicago,* 550; Rakeffet-Rothkoff, *Silver Era,* 325. Ephraim Epstein was very similar to Silver in his values and actions.

9. On this and following see "Epstein, Moses Mordecai," *Encyclopaedia Judaica,* 835 (year of birth is listed as 1866); Harry H. Epstein, "Rabbi Moshe Mordecai Epstein: A Sage and a Leader in Israel," in *Judaism and Progress: Sermons and Addresses* (New York: Bloch, 1935): "Slobodka Yeshiva," *Encyclopaedia Judaica,* 1668–69; "Lithuania," Ibid., 374–80.

10. On this and following, see Epstein/Bauman interview; Harry H. Epstein, "My tribute to a distinguished father," 3 December 1943, in "Friday Night Sermons and Related Materials" folder. On rabbinic aloofness, other defense mechanisms, and ways of maintaining role expectations, see Jacob Bloom, "The Rabbi as Symbolic Exemplar" (Ph.D. diss., Columbia University, 1972). On Lookstein, see Jenna Weissman Joselit, *New York's Jewish Jews: The Orthodox Community in the Interwar Years* (Bloomington and Indianapolis: Indiana University Press, 1990), 66–67.

Chapter 2. Growing Up

1. Epstein/Bauman interview: Davida and Renana Epstein, "To Grandpa on his Eightieth Birthday," 17 October 1956, in "Ephraim Epstein" folder; Chicago *Sun-Times,* 15 July 1960.

2. *American Jewish Yearbook,* cited in Meites, *Chicago,* 200 and Preface; Ira Berkow, *Maxwell Street: Survival in a Bazaar* (Garden City, N.Y.: Doubleday, 1977).

3. Epstein/Bauman interview: *Southern Israelite,* 24 November 1972; "Eighty-Fifth Anniversary of Ahavath Achim and Forty-Fifth Anniversary of Rabbi Harry Epstein Program;" Mishkin, "Epstein Story;" interview of Rabbi Harry H. Epstein by Cliff Kuhn (circa 1985) (hereafter cited as Epstein/Kuhn interview). According to the rabbi's recollection, Mrs. Zimmerman was related to the Zimmerman family so important to Atlanta's Congregation Shearith Israel. Kenneth W. Stein, *A History of the Ahavath Achim Synagogue, 1887–1977* (Atlanta: Standard Press, 1978), 31–32; Oscar Z. Fasman was an H.T.C. graduate who served in Tulsa's B'nai Emunah in 1930 and later became the college president. Fasman, "After Fifty Years, An Optimist," *American Jewish History* (December 1979), 159–73. He describes how Midwestern, Western and Southern congregations adopted the "modern Orthodox" designation in the 1930s in recognition of mixed seating and changed to "traditional" during the late 1940s (p. 162). See Jonathan D. Sarna, "The Debate Over Mixed Seating in the American Synagogue," Jack Wertheimer, ed., *The American Synagogue: A Sanctuary Transformed* (New York: Cambridge University Press, 1987), 363–94; Jeffrey S. Gurock, *The Men and Women of Yeshiva: Higher Education, Orthodoxy, and American Judaism* (New York: Columbia University Press, 1989).

4. Epstein/Bauman interview; Harry H. Epstein, "Dr. Bernard Revel—Builder of American Jewry," 6 December 1940, "Friday Night Sermons and Related Materials" folder; Louis Bernstein, "Generational Conflict in American Orthodoxy: The Early Years of the Rabbinical Council of America," *American Jewish History* (Decem-

ber 1979); 226–33; Bernstein, "The Emergence of the English Speaking Orthodox Rabbinate," (Ph.D. diss., Bernard Revel Graduate School of Yeshiva University, 1977); Raphael, *Profiles;* Gurock, "Resisters and Accommodators"; idem., *Men and Women of Yeshiva;* Gilbert Klaperman, *The Story of Yeshiva University: The First Jewish University in America* (London: Macmillan, 1969); Aaron Rothkoff, *Bernard Revel: Builder of American Jewish Orthodoxy* (Philadelphia: Jewish Publication Society, 1972); Sidney B. Hoenig, *The Scholarship of Dr. Bernard Revel* (New York: Yeshiva University Press, 1968); Alex J. Goldman, *Giants of Faith: Great American Rabbis* (New York: Citadel Press, 1964); Helmreich, *World of the Yeshiva,* chap. 2. Revel was from Kovno. He learned Musar at the Yeshiva where he and Rabbi Finkel's son were study mates. The latter (Abraham Finkel) was the future leader of the Hebron yeshiva. Rothkoff, *Revel,* 27–31.

5. Epstein/Bauman interview; Epstein, "Bernard Revel"; Bernstein, "Generational Conflict," 231.

6. Bernstein, "Generational Conflict"; Gurock, "Resisters and Accommodators;" Rakeffet-Rothkoff, *Silver Era;* Joselit, *New York's Jewish Jews;* Sarna, "Debate Over Mixed Seating"; Raphael, *Profiles;* Klaperman, *Yeshiva University;* Mark K. Bauman and Arnold Shankman, "The Rabbi as Ethnic Broker: The Case of David Marx," *Journal of American Ethnic History* (Spring 1983), 51–68. One of the factors influencing Ephraim Epstein may have been the very negative experience of Rabbi Willovsky, M. M. Epstein's brother-in-law, and one of the rabbis who granted Ephraim ordination. Willovsky, serving as chief rabbi of several Chicago congregations in 1903, resigned within a year over a disagreement concerning the supervision of kosher butchers. Aaron Rothkoff, "The American Sojourn of Ridbaz: Religious Problems Within the Immigrant Community," *American Jewish Historical Quarterly* (June 1968), 557–72.

7. On this and following, see Epstein/Bauman interview; Harry H. Epstein, "The Yeshiva in Slobodka," April 1924, reprinted in Epstein, *Judaism and Progress,* 283–87; Epstein, "M. M. Epstein." Epstein called the yeshiva "the greatest sanctuary of Jewish learning of the present age" (p. 266). Zachariah Shuster was a student at the Slobodka yeshiva for a short time in 1920. He was involved in the Maskil and secular learning. He became a journalist and longtime worker for the American Jewish Committee, who, nonetheless, appears to have gained considerably from the yeshiva way of thinking. Marc C. Tanenbaum, "Zachariah Shuster—A Moral Giant," typescript eulogy delivered at Riverside Chapel, New York, 17 February 1986. Stein, *Ahavath Achim,* 33; (Aaron) David Epstein to Harry H. Epstein, 5 August 1929, Epstein scrapbooks. On education in the yeshivot and seminaries, see Charles S. Liebman, "Training of American Rabbis," 6–11.

8. Epstein/Bauman interview; Harry H. Epstein's Ahavath Achim Bulletin articles, 26 January 1979, 2 February 1979.

9. Epstein/Bauman interview; "Kook (Kuk), Abraham Isaac," *Encyclopaedia Judaica,* vol. 10, 1182–87; Jacob B. Angus, *High Priest of Rebirth: The Life, Times, and Thought of Abraham Isaac Kuk* (New York: Bloch, 1946, 2d ed. 1972); Angus, "Abraham Isaac Kuk (1865–1935)," in Simon Novak, ed., *Great Jewish Thinkers of the Twentieth Century* (n.p.: B'nai Brith Department of Adult Education, 1963), 73–96; idem., "Orthodox Stream," 115–19. Angus describes Kook as an eclectic mystic who intertwined doubt and truth, and synthesized spiritualism and secular humanism.

10. Cliff Kuhn interview and manuscript, p. 54; Epstein/Bauman interview. Fund-raising drives like that undertaken by M. M. Epstein were not unusual. In 1924 he spearheaded a million-dollar drive with Rabbis Kook and Abraham Dov-Ber Kahane-Shapiro for Palestinian and European yeshivas sponsored by the Central

Committee for the Relief of Jewish War Sufferers. Rothkoff, "Last Rabbi of Kovno," 38.

11. Emory University Commencement Program, 1932; "Academic Course Work" folders; Harry H. Epstein, "The Basis of Religious Certainty in Judaism: A Study of Six Sources" (M.A. thesis, Emory University, 1932).

12. Epstein/Bauman interview; "Academic Studies-Philosophy" folder.

13. Epstein/Bauman interview; *Atlanta Journal,* 1 June 1963 (clipping inscribed by W. B. Baker), Epstein scrapbooks; Chapel address, 24 February 1941; Emory Jewish Student Forum, 29 October 1942; Emory Christian Association, 10 February 1943; Emory Jewish Students, 23 December 1946; Emory Christian Association Dinner, 6 May 1953; Emory Bible 101, 5 April 1954; Jack Boozer to Harry Epstein, 28 September 1956; Emory Hillel—Religious Emphasis Week, 11 November 1959, all in "Activities—Emory University" folder; January 1947, Epstein scrapbook. Epstein became Emory's first Hillel adviser when Hillel replaced the Jewish Students' Forum. *Southern Israelite,* 26 December 1986.

14. Ahavath Achim Bulletin, 27 February 1953; *Southern Israelite,* 27 February 1953; *Atlanta Journal,* 28 February 1953; "Epstein, Harry Hyman," *Who's Who in World Jewry* (Tel Aviv: Olive Books, 1955), 184; *Knoxville Journal,* 28 April 1949.

Chapter 3. The First Full-Time Pulpit

1. Fort Worth/Dallas, *Jewish Monitor,* 17 June 1927.

2. Epstein/Bauman interview; *Southern Israelite,* 3 September 1982; notes on Tulsa sermon, "Studies in Leadership," May 1927, "Activities—Tulsa, Oklahoma, 1927" folder. This sermon was refined and published in the Fort Worth/Dallas *Jewish Monitor,* Tulsa "Messenger" section, 9 September 1927. Epstein's sermon notes frequently are not written in sentence form. I have chosen to "fill in the blanks," so to speak, here and throughout, to facilitate reading, without changing the usually obvious meaning.

3. Epstein/Bauman interview; Epstein, "Studies in Leadership"; Epstein, "A Rabbi in Israel," in Epstein, *Judaism and Progress,* 203–16; cf. Bloom, "Rabbi as Symbolic Exemplar."

4. Epstein/Bauman interview; Epstein, "How Much Do We Weigh?" *Tulsa Tribune,* 5 May 1928. Epstein was given the substantial salary of $5,000 by the wealthy congregation. Simon Selinger to Epstein, 12 May 1927. For the relationship between the Travis family and Revel, and Revel's relationship to this congregation, see Rothkoff, *Revel.*

5. Epstein/Bauman interview; *The Fulton Fellowcraft,* 15 June 1946, Epstein scrapbooks; numerous civigraphs, 22 February 1972, Epstein scrapbooks; *Atlanta Georgian,* 25 March 1939.

Chapter 4. Ahavath Achim and Modern Orthodoxy

1. On this and following, see Stein, *Ahavath Achim;* Steven Hertzberg, *Strangers Within the Gate City, Jews of Atlanta,* 1845–1915 (Philadelphia: Jewish Publication Society, 1978); Solomon Sutker, "The Jews of Atlanta, Their Social Structure and Leadership Patterns" (Ph.D. diss., University of North Carolina, 1950); Janice O. Rothschild, *As But a Day: The First Hundred Years, 1867–1967* (Atlanta: Hebrew Benevolent Congregation, 1967); Mark K. Bauman, "Centripetal and Centrifugal Forces Facing the People of Many Communities: Atlanta Jewry from the Leo Frank

Case to the Great Depression," *Atlanta Historical Journal* (Fall 1979), 25–54; Bauman, "The Emergence of Jewish Social Service Agencies in Atlanta," *Georgia Historical Quarterly* (Winter 1985), 488–508; Bauman, "Role Theory and History: Ethnic Brokerage in the Atlanta Jewish Community," *American Jewish History* (September 1983), 71–95; Doris H. Goldstein, *From Generation to Generation: A Centennial History of Ahavath Achim, 1887–1987* (Atlanta: Capricorn, 1987); *Atlanta Constitution,* 12 August 1928. This last article reports that Ahavath Achim had more than twenty-five hundred members. Presumably, this figure represented individuals and not family memberships as recognized by Jewish congregations.

2. Gurock, "Resisters and Accommodators"; Sklare, *Conservative Judaism,* chap. 2 (for three areas of settlement model).

3. Raphael, *Profiles;* Gurock, "Resisters and Accommodators"; Bernstein, "Generational Conflict"; Epstein/Bauman interview; Stein, *History of Ahavath Achim;* telephone interview of Mrs. Doris Goldstein by this author, 12 August 1986 (Goldstein gathered information on Hirmes through conversations with his son, Eliezer Hirmes, and Rabbi Yitchak Rosenbaum, director of rabbinic alumni of Yeshiva Universty); David Geffen, "The Literary Legacy of Rabbi Tobias Geffen in Atlanta, 1910–1970," *Atlanta Historical Journal* (Fall 1979), 85–90; Nathan Kaganoff, "An Orthodox Rabbinate in the South: Tobias Geffen, 1870–1970," *American Jewish History* (September 1983), 56–70; telephone interview with David Geffen by this author, 10 October 1986. Geffen was born in Kovno.

There is a poignant aside to Hirmes's story. Klaperman (*Yeshiva University,* p. 104) lists an Abraham Hirmes as a student who explained the 1908 strike at R.I.E.T.S. to local congregations. The students struck unsuccessfully for more English, secular learning, and professional rabbinic training to augment the curriculum and better prepare them to meet the needs of an acculturating Orthodox community. Since Hirmes did not graduate until 1918, it is possible that he was one of the student leaders not allowed to return, and that he reentered when Bernard Revel became president and reorganized the school curriculum in accordance with the same philosophy.

4. On generational change and accommodation, see Deborah Dash Moore, *At Home in America; Second Generation New York Jews* (New York: Columbia University Press, 1981), especially 124, 138–40; Jeffrey S. Gurock, *When Harlem Was Jewish, 1870–1930* (New York: Columbia University Press, 1979). These parallels are drawn more clearly in my "Harry H. Epstein and the Adaptation of Second Generation East European Jews in Atlanta," *American Jewish Archives* (Fall/Winter 1990), 133–46.

5. On this and following, see Raphael, *Profiles,* 85–87; Sklare, *Conservative Judaism;* Gurock, "Resisters and Accommodators"; "Orthodoxy," *Encyclopaedia Judaica,* 1488–93; Eugene Markovitz, "Henry Pereira Mendes: Architect of the Union of Orthodox Jewish Congregations of America," *American Jewish Historical Quarterly* (March 1966), 364–84; Bernstein, "Emergence"; Ismar Schorsch, "Zacharias Frankel and the European Origins of Conservative Judaism," *Judaism* (Summer 1981), 344–54; Leo Jung, *The Path of a Pioneer: The Autobiography of Leo Jung* (New York: Soncino, 1980); Mel Scult, "The Sociologist as Theologian: The Fundamental Assumptions of Mordecai Kaplan's Thought," *Judaism* (Summer 1976), 345–52; Richard Libowitz, "Mordecai M. Kaplan as Redactor" (Ph.D.diss., Temple University, 1978); Ira Eisenstein and Eugene Kohn, *Mordecai M. Kaplan: An Evaluation* (New York: Reconstructionist Press, 1952); Eisenstein, "Mordecai M. Kaplan (1881–)," in Noveck, ed., *Great Jewish Thinkers,* 253–79; *Chicago Sun-Times,* 7 October 1929; *Chicago Sentinel,* 4 October 1956; "Ephraim Epstein" folder. Joseph P. Schultz indicates that the Hebrew Theological College was a training institute for modern

Orthodox rabbis in "The Consensus of 'Civil Religion': The Religious Life of Kansas City Jewry," Schultz, ed., *Mid-America's Promise: A Profile of Kansas City Jewry* (Kansas City, Mo.: Jewish Community Foundation of Greater Kansas City and American Jewish Historical Society, 1982), 42.

I think that both Raphael and Sklare are too institutionally oriented in their delineations of Conservative and Orthodox Judaism. Although their dating of Conservatism as a movement may be accurate, it is equally appropriate to trace the antecedents of the ideology, however ill defined, varied, and problematic it may have been, to nineteenth-century sources. See the special issue of *American Jewish History* (December 1984) on Sklare; Davis, *Emergence of Conservative Judaism*, Abraham J. Karp, "The Conservative Rabbi—Dissatisfied But Not Unhappy," in Sarna, ed., "The American Rabbinate," 188–262; Sussman, "Leeser," 414 (for term *"problematic"*).

Raphael (*Profiles*, 147–49) has associated the Agudath HaRabbonim with rabbis from Kovno. Kovno was also the home of such diverse individuals as Bernard Revel, Bernard Levinthal, and Saul Silber, a key president of the Hebrew Theological College of Chicago. Aaron Kotler and the Soloveitchek family were associated with the city and Slobodka suburb. Eliezar Silver, born in a town in Kovno in 1881, represented the American equivalent to Hildesheimer during the first half of the twentieth century. This area and its yeshivot had a profound impact on American Orthodoxy and Conservatism, and it would be a fertile field for additional study. See also the sketches in Goldman, *Giants of Faith*.

David Ellenson, "Rabbi Esriel Hildesheimer and the Quest for Religious Authority: The Earliest Years," *Modern Judaism* (December 1981), 279–97; idem., "A Response by Modern Orthodoxy to Jewish Religious Pluralism: The Case of Esriel Hildesheimer," *Tradition* (Spring 1979), 74–90; I. Harold Sharfman, *The First Rabbi: Origins of Conflict Between Orthodox and Reform: Jewish Polemic Warfare in Pre-Civil War America* (n.p.: Joseph Simon/Pangloss, 1988); Sussman, "Leeser"; Gurock, in *Men and Women of Yeshiva University*, 36–37, indicates that Reines attempted to mix traditional and secular studies at the Lida yeshiva in Russia; idem., "From Exception to Role Model: Bernard Drachman and the Evolution of Jewish Religious Life in America, 1880–1920," *American Jewish History* (June 1987), 456–84. Joselit's *New York's Jewish Jews* became available late in the revision stages of this volume, but it proved to be invaluable.

6. On this and following, see Epstein/Bauman interview; Epstein/Kuhn interview; Stein, *Ahavath Achim; Chicago Chronicle*, 18 January 1929.

7. On this and following, see Lena Goldberg eulogy, *Southern Israelite*, 30 August 1940, and issues of 17 June 1938 and 17 September 1936; "Book Reviews" folder; Bible Class, 9 December 1928, "Chanukah—Speeches" folder; Souvenir Program, Dedicated to the Ahavath Achim Synagogue Center by the Synagogue Brotherhood, 16 April 1940; *Atlanta Georgian*, 20 June 1938; Brotherhood Banquet, 22 November 1935, "Friday Night" folder; Harry H. Epstein to Mr. Friedman, 26 October 1932, "A. A. Brotherhood" folder; Orin Borsten, "Modernizing Traditional Judaism;" *Atlanta Constitution*, 29 November 1930, 20 October 1934, and 13 November 1932; New Orleans *Morning Tribune*, 27 February 1935; Harry H. Epstein to Levin, 27 January 1935, "Activities—New Orleans" folder; Epstein/Bauman interview; Epstein/Kuhn interview. It is possible that Mordecai Kaplan's daughter was this country's first bat mitzvah in 1922. Murray Polner, *Rabbi: The American Experience* (New York: Holt, Rinehart and Winston, 1977), 152. Epstein's daughter's was one of the first in his congregation. Carolyn Gold, "When Bat Mitzvahs Began," *Southern Israelite*, 18 July 1986.

Gershom Hadas moved his Kansas City congregation Kneseth Israel–Beth Shalom from modern Orthodoxy to Conservatism during his tenure from 1929 to 1963, much as did Epstein. Bella E. Schultz, "Transmitting the Heritage: Jewish Education in Kansas City," Schultz, ed., *Mid-America's Promise,* 63. Ironically, Hadas had been one of Tobias Geffen's yeshiva students.

8. On Kaplan's innovations and the synagogue center, see sources in n.56 above and Moore, *At Home in America;* Aaron I. Reichel, *The Maverick Rabbi: Rabbi Herbert S. Goldstein and the Institutional Synagogue—"A New Institutional Form"* (Norfolk, Va.: Donning, 1984).

9. On this and following, see Twenty-Fifth Anniversary Program, 19 October 1960; Louis Silverman to Harry H. Epstein; speech notes, Installation of Rabbi A. J. Mesch, 1935; Tenth Anniversary Testimonial, 6 February 1946; speech notes, Rabbi Mesch's Twentieth Anniversary, 27 April 1955, all in "Activities—Birmingham" folder; *Birmingham News,* 11 March 1937; telephone interviews with Mrs. Vellie Mesch, the rabbi's wife, by this author, 17 November 1986 and 24 November 1986, and with Dr. Barry Mesch, his son, 15 November 1986; Mark H. Elovitz, *A Century of Jewish Life in Dixie: The Birmingham Experience* (Tuscaloosa: University of Alabama Press, 1974), 90–95, 99–101, 139–53, 163–65, 168–69; Southeast Regional Program, 8–9 April 1956, "United Synagogue of America" folder.

10. Hirsch Heiman to Harry H. Epstein, 11 March 1938, 3 April 1938; Golden Anniversary, Knesset Israel, 1888–1938, Program, "Activities—Minneapolis, Minnesota" folder.

11. See Moore, *At Home in America,* for a similar interpretation. For the similar experiences of Rabbis Abraham M. Hershman in Detroit and Saul E. White in San Francisco, Robert A. Rockaway, *The Jews of Detroit, From the Beginning, 1762–1914* (Detroit: Wayne State University Press, 1986), 75–78; Michael M. Zarchin, *Glimpses of Jewish Life in San Francisco* (Oakland, Calif.: Judah L. Magnes Memorial Museum, 1952, rev. ed., 1964), 138–39; Joselit, *New York's Jewish Jews.*

12. Epstein kept virtually all of his sermons and sermon notes. See, for example, "Difference Between Reform and Orthodoxy," 29 November 1935, "Friday Night" folder; Tulsa, 1927, "Devorim" folder; "Conservative Judaism" folder throughout; Ahavath Achim History, 1954; Ahavath Achim Sisterhood Souvenir Journal, 1953; *Southern Israelite,* 17 September 1936. The Epstein scrapbooks include numerous accounts of his speeches in other cities. See, for example, *Union of American Hebrew Congregations Monthly,* March 1935; Rabbi Silber T. Rand to Ahavath Achim, 2 September 1928; *Savannah Morning News,* 17 October 1937.

Chapter 5. Reaching Out to Different Communities

1. *Miami Herald,* 1 March 1936; Bauman, "Emergence of Jewish Social Services"; Stein, *Ahavath Achim,* 28–29; sermons, 21 April 1932, 3 March 1953, 27 March 1956, 6 April 1958; "Passover Sermons" folder; sermon, 20 March 1953, "Friday Sermons" folder.

2. Epstein realized the need for traditional Jewish community structures. He supported the building of a *mikveh* in 1935 and worked with Rabbi Tobias Geffen of Shearith Israel regulating ritual slaughter, even though the latter duty proved distasteful. At one point, for example, Epstein knew that the necessary denunciation from the pulpit of one butcher would drive the man out of business. An older and longer-established leader, Geffen protected his *kashruth* prerogative and, for many years, was condescending to the younger man. This generational conflict was typical, although fees may not have been involved as they were in other cities since Geffen may not have accepted them. See Rakeffet-Rothkoff, *Silver Era;* "Mikveh"

folder; Epstein/Bauman interview; pamphlet by Epstein and Geffen on closing kosher butchers and delicatessens on the Sabbath, Epstein scrapbooks.

3. On this and following, see *Savannah Morning News,* 19 November 1943;
Bauman, "Emergence of Jewish Social Services"; Bauman, "Role Theory and His-
tory"; Sutker, "Jews of Atlanta"; 19 April 1936, 20 December 1938, "Jewish Welfare
Federation—Campaign" folder; "Penintentiary" folder; *Atlanta Constitution,* 17
April 1936, 21 March 1950, 15 March 1962; *Augusta Chronicle,* 28 March 1948;
Southern Israelite, 3 February 1950, 31 March 1950, 15 March 1946; *Atlanta Journal,*
21 March 1950; "Welfare Federation Sabbath," 19 April 1948, "Friday Night" folder;
sermon, 15 February 1980, "Friday Night" folder; Ahavath Achim Brotherhood
Souvenir Program, 16 April 1940. On Rothschild, see Janice Rothschild Blumberg,
One Voice: Rabbi Jacob M. Rothschild and the Troubled South (Macon, Ga.: Mercer
University Press, 1985). David Marx, Rothschild's predecessor, had helped create
Atlanta's Jewish social services. See Bauman, "Emergence of Jewish Social Services"; interview of Max ("Mike") Gettinger, former director of the Atlanta Jewish
Federation, by this author, 16 June 1986. Epstein was the first Orthodox rabbi to
gain Marx's respect and a relative amount of acceptance. On Marx, see Bauman and
Shankman, "Rabbi as Ethnic Broker"; Epstein/Bauman interview. The campaign
director of the Atlanta Jewish Welfare Fund wrote Epstein, "You are the logical
leader in this state of all the conservative and orthodox [*sic*] groups. This naturally
implies a responsibility and I do hope that you will give freely of your gifts to
Atlanta and the rest of the state as well as the adjacent cities like Birmingham and
Montgomery." Arthur Adams to Harry H. Epstein, 22 April 1936, "Correspondence—English" folder. On the importance of B'nai B'rith as an integrating agency,
see William Toll, *The Making of an Ethnic Middle Class: Portland Jewry over Four
Generations* (Albany: State University of New York Press, 1982).

4. *Atlanta Constitution,* 18 February 1937, 20 June 1953; *A.D.L. Review,* 19
October 1939; civigraphs, 22 February 1972; *Southern Israelite,* 3 September 1982,
25 January 1963; *Asheville Citizen–Times,* 15 November 1936; "Golden Jubilee, 2
November 1975, Jewish Theological Seminary"; United Synagogue of America
Seaboard Region, subregional conference, Temple Israel, Charlotte, N.C., (n.d.);
Greenville (S.C.) *News,* April 1964; Southern Branch, National Women's League,
U.S.A., Beth-El, Birmingham, 15 January 1956; "Activities—Birmingham" folder;
"United Synagogue of America" folder; Epstein's thirty-fifth anniversary, Ahavath
Achim Testimonial Issue, 3 June 1963; dedication program, Southeast Region Rab-
binical Association, 2 May 1965; "Activities—Macon" folder.

5. "Derelicts in Life" (circa 1935), "Friday Night" folder; "Palestine—The Jewish Homeland," Lions Club, Fall 1929, "Zionism" folder; Hadassah donor dinner,
27 May 1951, "Activities—Mobile" folder; Arnold M. Eisen, *Galut: Modern Jewish
Reflection on Homelessness and Homecoming* (Bloomington: Indiana University Press,
1986); Allon Gal, "The Mission Motif in American Zionism (1898–1948)," *American
Jewish History* (June 1986), 41–64.

6. On this and following, see Sermons, 26 September 1957, 27 September 1946,
"High Holidays" folder; "Israel's Bar Mitzvah Year," 21 April 1960, "Friday Night"
folder; Melvin I. Urofsky, "A Cause in Search of Itself: American Zionism After
the State," *American Jewish History* (December 1979), 85.

7. Sermons, 3 November 1967, 3 May 1968, 24 January 1969, 19 December
1969, 18 October 1974, 15 November 1974, 7 March 1976, 9 April 1976, 17 August
1979, 7 September 1979, 13 August 1982, "Friday Night" folder; sermon, 13 April
1968, "Passover" folder.

8. Melvin I. Urofsky, *American Zionism from Herzl to the Holocaust* (Garden
City, N.Y.: Doubleday, 1975); *idem.,* "A Cause in Search of Itself," 79–91; *idem.,*

A Voice That Spoke for Justice: The Life and Times of Stephen A. Wise (Albany: State University of New York Press, 1982); idem., *We Are One! American Jewry and Israel* (Garden City, N.Y.: Doubleday, 1978); Peter Grose, *Israel in the Mind of America* (New York: Knopf, 1983); Zvi Ganin, *Truman, American Jewry and Israel, 1945–1948* (New York: Holmes and Meier, 1979); Ben Halpern, *The Idea of a Jewish State* (Cambridge: Harvard University Press, 2d ed., 1961); Samuel Halpern, *The Political World of American Zionism* (Detroit: Wayne State University Press, 1961); Arthur Hertzberg, *The Zionist Idea* (New York: Herzl Press and Doubleday, 1959); Eisen, *Galut;* Gal, "Mission Motif," 363–85; Raphael Patai, *Tents of Jacob: The Diaspora— Yesterday and Today* (Englewood Cliffs, N.J.: Prentice-Hall, 1971).

9. On this and following, see Palestine Evening Program, 23 December 1928; telegram, 6 September 1929, Epstein scrapbooks; *Atlanta Journal* 20 March 1929, 27 August 1929, 1 September 1929; *Southern Israelite,* 20 March 1929, 30 August 1929; radio address, 8 September 1929; "Palestine—The Jewish Homeland," Atlanta Lions Club speech, Fall 1929; Jewish Women's Club Mass meeting (n.d.), all in "Zionism" folder; Harry H. Epstein, *Judaism and Progress,* chap. 14; Naomi W. Cohen, *The Year after the Riots: American Response to the Palestine Crisis of 1929–1930* (Detroit: Wayne State University Press, 1987). Sokolow was the president of the Council of the Rights of Jewish Minorities, forerunner of the World Jewish Congress. Urofsky, *Voice That Spoke for Justice,* 294.

10. On this and following, see unidentified newspaper clipping, 8 July 1929, Epstein scrapbooks; *Atlanta Journal,* 10 June 1935; radio addresses and speeches, 21 May 1935, 26 May 1935, 13 March 1932, 18 November 1936, 23 September 1940, 4 October 1937, 12 April 1938, 23 September 1940, 19–21 November 1943, 23 April 1944, 24 April 1944, 2 April 1946; "Zionism as Affirmation of Judaism," "A statement of 757 Orthodox, Conservative and Reform Rabbis of America to a statement issued by Ninety Members of the Reform Rabbinate charging that Zionism is Incompatible with the Teachings of Judaism," American Emergency Committee for Zionist Affairs, 1942, all in "Zionism" folder; sermons, 3 March 1939, 1 November 1935, 2 January 1941, 23 October 1942, "Friday Night" folder; "J.N.F." folder; *Southern Israelite,* 26 April 1940; speech, 4 June 1940; "Activities— Charlotte" folder; speech, 14 April 1940, "Activities—Augusta, Ga." folder; sermon, 19 May 1939, "Passover Services" folder; speech, 27 April 1939, "Activities— Greenville, S.C." folder; speeches, 3 May 1936, 12 May 1936, "Junior Hadassah" folder; Epstein/Bauman interview; Sarah Schmidt, "Horace M. Kallen and the 'Americanization' of Zionism: In Memoriam," *American Jewish Archives* (April 1976), 68, 70; Melvin I. Urofsky, *Louis D. Brandeis and the Progressive Tradition* (Boston: Little, Brown, 1981). On Bublick, see Urofsky, *Voice That Spoke for Justice,* 127. Bublick witnessed the Palestine disturbances and reported on them at a rally at Ahavath Achim. *Atlanta Journal,* 8 December 1929.

11. Sermon, 10 September 1934, "High Holidays" folder: "Is There a Reason for Persecution?" 6 December 1935, report on National Conference for Palestine, 7 February 1935; report on Zionist district meeting, 23 September 1940, "Zionism" folder; sermons, 3 March 1939, 1 March 1940, 13 October 1939, 20 December 1939, 3 November 1939, 2 January 1941, 23 October 1942, 11 December 1942, "Friday Night" folder; sermons, 7 April 1936, 4 April 1939, 23 April 1940, 2 April 1942, 20 April 1943, 15 April 1944, "Passover Sermons" folder; Yehuda Bauer, *My Brother's Keepers: A History of the American Jewish Joint Distribution Committee, 1929–1939* (Philadelphia: Jewish Publication Society, 1974); Handlin, *A Continuing Task;* speeches dated 1959, 1963, 1964, 1969, and 9 May 1972, as well as talk before regional Women's O.R.T. Board, 7 May 1974, "O.R.T." folder; Leon Shapiro, *The History of O.R.T.* (Hoboken, N.J.: KTAV, 1980); Jack Rader, *By the Skill of Their*

Hands: The Story of O.R.T. (Geneva: World O.R.T. Union, 1970); Marc Lee Raphael, *Abba Hillel Silver: A Profile in American Judaism* (New York and London: Holmes and Meier, 1989).

12. For this and following, see report on National Conference for Palestine, 1–2 February 1936; sermons and speeches, 7 February 1936, 17 November 1939, 26 April 1940, 13 August 1943, 14 January 1944, "Zionism" folder; *Southern Israelite,* 31 January 1936; *Savannah Morning News,* 24 October 1939, 19 November 1943; telegrams, William F. Rose to Harry H. Epstein, 28 January 1948, Jonah B. Wise to Harry H. Epstein, 18 April 1940, Stephen S. Wise to Harry H. Epstein, 30 November 1938; *The Voice of Congregation Chevra Thilim,* San Francisco, July 1943, Epstein scrapbooks; *Miami Herald,* 28 December 1938; *Atlanta Journal,* 6 January 1939. Electors from all Jewish organizations in Atlanta convened to vote from among Julian V. Boehm, from the German subcommunity, Rabbi Joseph I. Cohen, from the Sephardic subcommunity, and Harry Epstein for the 1942 conference. Epstein won by a large margin. The vote signified the dominance of his group in the city. The individual vote tally is in Epstein scrapbooks. Eighth Annual Conference of the Southeast Zionist Region Program, 25–28 January 1946; *The Fulton Fellowcraft,* 15 June 1946; Melvin I. Urofsky, "Cause in Search of Itself"; Marc Lee Raphael, *A History of the United Jewish Appeal,* 1939–1982 (Chico, Calif.: Scholars Press, 1982). See also speeches, 18 April 1945, "Activities—Jacksonville" folder; 27 May 1951, "Activities—Mobile" folder; 24 January 1937, 6 March 1946, "Mizrachi" folder; sermons, 22 February 1946, 1 November 1935, "Friday Night" folder; 30 September 1943, 15 September 1947, "High Holidays" folder; 27 April 1943, 7 December 1947, 23 May 1964, "Special Services" folder; *Southern Israelite,* 21 March 1950, 31 March 1950, 23 October 1970, 21 February 1971, 24 May 1986; Mendel H. Fisher to Harry H. Epstein, 20 January 1958, "J.N.F." folder; speech, 18 November 1963, "O.R.T." folder; *Atlanta Constitution,* 8 January 1971, 26 January 1974; speech, 14 May 1985, "Israel" folder; sermon, 10 April 1971, "Passover" folder.

Epstein also supported efforts to relocate refugees after the war. Ultimately, more than 140 families were settled in Atlanta, especially through the resolve of the Ahavath Achim sisterhood. Harry H. Epstein to Dear Friends, 16 March 1950, Kuhn manuscripts; Herte Sanders interview by Cliff Kuhn, (n.d.).

13. On this and following, see Epstein/Bauman interview. The current debate over the Holocaust and American Jewish actions and responsibility is extensive. See, for example, David S. Wyman, *The Abandonment of the Jews: America and the Holocaust, 1941–1945* (New York: Pantheon, 1984); Yehuda Brauer, *American Jewry and the Holocaust* (Detroit: Wayne State University Press, 1981); Raphael Medloff, *The Deafening Silence: American Jewish Leaders and the Holocaust* (New York: Shapolsky, 1987); Edward Pinsky, "American Jewish Unity During the Holocaust—The Joint Emergency Committee, 1943," *American Jewish History* (June 1983); Henry L. Feingold, "Courage First and Intelligence Second: The American Jewish Secular Elite, Roosevelt and the Failure to Rescue," *American Jewish History* (June 1983), 424–60.

14. On the concept of community builder, see Mark K. Bauman, "Victor H. Kriegshaber, Community Builder," *American Jewish History* (Autumn 1989). See also Bauman and Shankman, "Rabbi as Ethnic Broker," and idem., "Role Theory and History."

15. On this and following, see Epstein/Bauman interview; WSB radio addresses, 4 November 1928, 3 March 1929, "Radio Addresses" folder; 4 November 1932, "WAGA TV Reflections" folder; *Atlanta Journal,* 17 February 1962; dedication program, The Chapel of All Faiths, Milledgeville State Hospital, 14 February 1964; Memorial Day Parade Program, 26 April 1934, Aaron Cohen to Harry H. Epstein,

8 February 1937; George T. Smith to Harry H. Epstein, 26 February 1964; Bill C. Wainwright to Harry H. Epstein, 23 December 1970; WSB radio WSBeaver Award, 12 February 1968, 9 February 1974, all in Epstein scrapbooks; *Atlanta Constitution,* 11 March 1935; *News Sun,* 24 May 1978; WGST radio "Church of the Air" program, 11 May 1947; "Church versus State," 1961, "Addresses, Misc." folder; 23 October 1950, "Activities—Marietta" folder. A *Southern Israelite* editorial (18 May 1929).

16. *Atlanta Constitution,* 14 October 1931, 13 October 1931, "Community Chest" folder; 20 November 1933, 11 October 1955, "Radio Addresses" folder.

17. On this and following, see 26 October 1938, WATL, "Radio Addresses" folder; 11 May 1947, "Addresses, Misc." folder; undated sermons, 1968(?), 1970(?), 1974(?), "Saturday Morning Sermons" folder; sermons, 23 September 1968, 26 October 1962, 2 November 1962, 16 November 1962, 30 November 1971, 19 June 1970, 12 November 1948, "Friday Night" folder; Epstein/Bauman interview; *Atlanta Journal,* 12 March 1953; *Atlanta Constitution,* 20 November 1964, 27 October 1963, 7 November 1965, "Adult Classes—Sunday Morning" folder. The bat mitzvah, or coming of age ceremony (usually at the age of twelve or thirteen) for a girl, heterosexual seating (as opposed to women sitting in a balcony, or separated area), and women's participation in services symbolized dramatic changes in the image and roles of women and, during the 1920s and 1930s, also tended to denote distinctions between Orthodox and Conservative congregations.

18. On this and following, see Marjorie McLachlan to Harry H. Epstein, 24 March 1948, 29 March 1948, 30 March 1948, "Brotherhood" folder; sermons, 12 November 1948, 4 March 1949, 24 February 1961, 18 October 1963, 22 November 1963, 26 March 1965, 7 October 1966, 14 October 1966, 14 March 1969, "Friday Night" folder; Jacob M. Rothschild to Harry H. Epstein, 3 December 1963, box 6, folder 3, Jacob M. Rothschild Collection, Special Collections, Woodruff Library, Emory University; sermon, 4 April 1969; *Atlanta Constitution,* 29 January 1974; speech, Emory Hillel—Religious Emphasis Week, 11 November 1959, "Emory" folder. On Southern rabbis and black civil rights, see Blumberg, *One Voice;* Mark Cowett, *Birmingham's Rabbi: Morris Newfield and Alabama, 1895–1940* (Tuscaloosa: University of Alabama Press, 1986); Malcolm Stern, "The Role of the Rabbi in the South," in Nathan Kaganoff and Melvin Urofsky, eds., *Turn to the South* (Charlottesville: University Press of Virginia for the American Jewish Historical Society, 1979), 21–31; Allen Krause, "Rabbis and Negro Rights in the South, 1954–1967," *American Jewish Archives* (1969), 20–47.

Chapter 6. The World of Ideas

1. On this and following, see *The Eternal Light* (New York: Harper and Row, 1966), 197 (full quote given in Epstein, *Judaism and Progress,* 219); 15 February 1929, 10 March 1929, 4 November 1932, "Religion" folder; speech, "Brotherhood in Theory and Action," 26 February 1960; "Brotherhood" folder; *Savannah Morning News,* 23 February 1931; sermons, undated, 1963(?); "Friday Night" folder; 1961(?), "Saturday Morning Sermons" folder.

2. Bible class, 9 December 1928, "Chanukah Speeches" folder; undated, 1961(?), "Saturday Morning Sermons" folder; *Chicago Jewish Daily Courier,* 13 March 1924; Harry H. Epstein, "In Quest of a Good Year: A New Year's Meditation," *Emory University Quarterly* (Winter 1962); *Savannah Morning News,* 16 December 1928; Harry H. Epstein, "How Much Do We Weigh?" *Tulsa Tribune,* 5 May 1928; speeches, Congregation Anshe Knesses Israel, November 1926, "Chanukah Speeches" folder; 8 February 1939, "Activities—Macon" folder.

3. Sermons, 13 November 1959, 20 March 1953, 16 October 1963, 14 January 1940, "Friday Night" folder.

4. Epstein's search for proof of God will be discussed below. On this and following, see Sermon, 3 April 1977, "Passover Sermons" folder; Raphael, *Profiles,* 85–87; Ginzburg, *Students, Scholars and Saints,* chap. 8; *The Eternal Light,* 45, 51, 98, 132, 163; speeches, 16 October 1938, 20 November 1938, "Jewish History" folder; sermon, 15 September 1956, "High Holidays" folder; Harry H. Epstein, "The Jewish Concept of Progress," Rosh Hashanah sermon, 21 September 1933, *Judaism and Progress* (especially p. 7); Epstein, "The Jewish Way to Progress," Rosh Hashanah sermon, 22 September 1933, *Judaism and Progress* (especially p. 25); "Sermon—The Jews and Progress, 1927," Tulsa Passover sermon; 1927 explanation of Deuteronomy portion, "Devorim" folder.

5. 16 October 1938, 20 November 1938, "Jewish History" folder; speech, Greater Miami Federation of Welfare Funds workers, 28 December 1938, "Activities—Miami" folder; speech, sisterhood adult education class, 5 March 1963, "Purim" folder; sermons, 30 December 1938, "Friday Night" folder; 13 April 1941, 13 April 1968, "Passover Sermons" folder.

6. Harry H. Epstein, "The Philosophy of Evolution," Emory University Biology 102, Spring 1931, term paper, "Academic Course Work—Evolution, 1931" folder; speeches, 9 January 1956, 1 February 1960, "Conservative Judaism" folder; "The Survival of the Morally Fittest," 21 February 1964, "Brotherhood" folder. For an example of the interaction between Christian ideas and a Reform rabbi, see Cowett, *Birmingham's Rabbi;* for Protestantism, evolution, and social thought, see Richard Hofstadter, *Social Darwinism in American Thought* (Philadelphia: University of Pennsylvania Press, 1944); Morton White, *Social Thought in America: The Revolt Against Formalism* (New York: Viking, 1947); Charles Howard Hopkins, *The Rise of the Social Gospel in American Protestantism* (New Haven: Yale University Press, 1940).

7. Sermons, 24 September 1968, 2 October 1968, 26 September 1973, 15 September 1966, 22 September 1941, 12 September 1942, 4 October 1940, "High Holidays sermons" folder; Harry H. Epstein, "The Meaning of Freedom," Passover sermon, 13 April 1930, 14 April 1930, *Judaism and Progress,* 149–56; undated sermon, 1969(?), "Saturday Morning Sermons" folder; sermons, 10 December 1948, 8 March 1946, 7 February 1947, "Friday Night" folder; speech, 16 June 1962, "Activities—Montreal" folder. Compare Epstein's attitude toward free will with Reinhold Niebuhr, *The Children of Light and the Children of Darkness* (New York: Charles Scribner's Sons, 1944).

8. On this and following, see speech, Rotary Club, 7 September 1944, "Activities—Griffin, Ga." folder; sermons, 9 October 1943, "High Holiday" folder; 7 April 1936, 4 April 1939, 23 April 1940, 20 April 1943, 8 April 1944, 29 April 1945, 16 April 1946, 5 April 1947, 2 April 1950, 31 March 1950, 27 March 1956, 19 March 1974, "Passover Sermons" folder; undated fragment, "Friday Night Misc. Notes" folder; 20 November 1964, "Friday Night" folder; 3 April 1938, "Activities—Minneapolis, Minn." folder. Epstein viewed religion as the best defense against communism. See *Atlanta Constitution,* 17 August 1953; Harry H. Epstein, "The Meaning of Freedom," Passover sermon, 13 April 1930, *Judaism and Progress,* 134–46. Much has been written about the interrelationship between religion and patriotism and about civil religion as well. See Jonathan S. Woocher, *Sacred Religion: The Civil Religion of American Jews* (Bloomington: Indiana University Press, 1986); Sidney Mead, *Lively Experiment* (New York: Harper and Row, 1963); William G. McLoughlin, *Modern Revivalism* (New York: Ronald, 1959). Historians of American Jewry have described how numerous rabbis served as chaplains during the world wars and helped raise funds in behalf of bond drives, as their willing congregants

138 Notes

volunteered for service. These historians have tended to emphasize Jewish service as an attempt to prove Jewish allegiance and to overcome any question of dual loyalty. Epstein, too, served as a chaplain and helped raise funds in Atlanta at a special Jewish rally to support the construction of the battleship named for the city during World War II. He was not, however, a blind jingoist. He evidently felt sufficiently secure to qualify his support and also was able to retain independent judgment.

9. On this and following, see Epstein/Bauman interview; sermons, 17 November 1946, 17 January 1947, 24 January 1947, 31 January 1947, 4 December 1956, "Prayer (Concept of)" folder; 1 January 1942, National Day of Prayer, "Services—Special" folder; "Academic Studies—Psychology of Jewish Worship, Fall 1931" folder; 15 December 1954, "Conservative Judaism" folder; Harry H. Epstein, "Divided Loyalties—The Jewish Dilemma," Jewish Educational Alliance, Savannah, Ga., 22 February 1931, *Judaism and Progress*, 115–16; "The Kabbalah," "Academic Studies—Mysticism, Fall 1929," folder; 6 December 1953, synagogue dedication speech, "Or Veshalom—Atlanta, Ga." folder; 6 January 1958, "Passover Sermons" folder; "Radio Speech, 9 December 1928, Atlanta, Ga., WSB Atlanta Broadcasting Station" folder.

10. On the divergent views between the rabbi and congregants concerning the role of the rabbi and sermons, and on conflicts noted below, see Bloom, "Rabbi as Symbolic Exemplar." On this and following, see 9 December 1956, "Activities—Montgomery, Ala." folder; Lisa Geldbart, "A Conversation with Rabbi Epstein," *Southern Israelite*, 24 March 1978; Harry H. Epstein, "A Rabbi in Israel," Ahavath Achim installation sermon, 2 September 1920, *Judaism and Progress*, 203–16; Epstein, "Studies in Leadership," B'nai Emunah installation sermon, 9 September 1927; Fort Worth/Dallas *Jewish Monitor*, Tulsa "Messenger" section, 13 September 1927; installation of Rabbi Abraham J. Mesch, 1935, 10th Anniversary Testimonial, 6 February 1946, 25th Anniversary, 16 October 1960, "Activities—Birmingham" folder; undated sermon, 1968(?), "Saturday Morning Sermons" folder; 7 December 1962, "Friday Night" folder; 14 January 1952, WSB radio, "Radio Addresses" folder.

11. See the fictional life of the rabbi/judge in Isaac Bashevis Singer, *In My Father's Court* (New York: Farrar, Straus and Giroux, 1966); "Arbitration, 1928–1948" folder. See concluding "Overview and Conclusion" for the role of the rabbi as judge.

12. For Epstein's frequent comparisons between Judaism and Hellenic culture, see "Chanukah—Speeches, etc., 1928–1979" folder; "Greek and Jew," Bible class, 9 December 1928; "Comparative Religion," 3 November 1932; "Why Religion?" 4 November 1932, 10 March 1929, "Religion" folder; 2 January 1981, "Friday Night" folder; 23 February 1951, 26 February 1960, "Brotherhood" folder; 5 April 1954, Bible 101, "Emory University" folder; 27 October 1954, "Conservative Judaism" folder.

13. Undated sermon, 1965(?), "Saturday Morning Sermons" folder; 16 June 1962, "Activities—Montreal, Ca.," folder; 6 April 1958, 27 March 1975, "Passover Sermons" folder; 20 September 1950, 20 September 1955, 29 September 1935, "High Holidays Sermons" folder; 16 October 1932, "Succoth" folder; cf. Arnold M. Eisen, *The Chosen People: A Study in Jewish Religious Ideology* (Bloomington: Indiana University Press, 1983).

14. On this and following, see Sermons, 17 October 1969, 27 March 1970, "Friday Night" folder; dedication program, 60th Anniversary of Sherah Israel, 2 May 1965, "Activities—Macon, Ga." folder; 2 November 1975, Golden Jubilee, Jewish

Theological Seminary; review, Meyer Levin's *In Search,* 22 January 1951, "Book Reviews" folder.

15. Bauman/Epstein interview; Daniel Elazar, *Community and Polity: The Organizational Dynamics of American Jewry* (Philadelphia: Jewish Publication Society, 1976). Jonathan D. Sarna describes the move from modern Orthodox to Conservative or traditional with reference to mixed seating, especially among Hebrew Theological College graduates, in "Debate Over Mixed Seating," 363–94; Joselit, *New York's Jewish Jews,* 66–67.

16. Bauman/Epstein interview; sermon, 29 November 1935, "Friday Night" folder; 1 December 1954, "Conservative Judaism" folder.

17. 4 October 1954, 1 December 1954, 13 November 1958, "Conservative Judaism" folder; Comparative Religion, 9 December 1954, "Central School of Religion Correspondence Courses" folder; Congregation Sherah Israel, Spring 1960, "Activities—Macon" folder.

18. On the impact of Orthodox rabbis after World War II, see Raphael, *Profiles;* Gurock, "Resisters and Accommodators."

19. A fourth colleague was Rabbi Joseph I. Cohen, but the Sephardic culture was just too divergent, and this subcommunity remained relatively isolated. Sol Beton, ed., *Sephardim and a History of Congregation of Veshalom* (Atlanta: Congregation Or VeShalom, 1981). Bauman/Epstein interview; Geffen interview; Ziff, ed., *Lev Tuviah;* Kaganoff, "Orthodox Rabbinate"; Geffen, "Literary Legacy"; Rothschild, *As But a Day;* Bauman and Shankman, "Rabbi as Ethnic Broker"; Blumberg, *One Voice;* Rakeffet-Rothkoff, *Silver Era;* Gurock, "Resisters and Accommodators"; Bernstein, "Emergence."

20. Mishkin interview; 7 January 1963, 5 November 1962, "Conservative Judaism" folder.

21. Epstein/Bauman interview.

22. Epstein/Bauman interview; Epstein, "Basis of Religious Certainty" (especially pp. 134–35). Epstein's thought closely resembles that of Milton Steinberg, although Steinberg was more influenced by Reconstructionism. See Simon Noveck, *Milton Steinberg: Portrait of a Rabbi* (New York: KTAV, 1978), as well as Jacob J. Weinstein, *Solomon Goldman: A Rabbi's Rabbi* (New York: KTAV, 1973).

23. On this and following, see several undated sermons, 1963–64(?), "Saturday Morning Sermons" folder; undated sermon, "What is Faith?," "Faith" folder; Bible class, 9 December 1927, "Chanukah speeches" folder; 3 December 1940, "Book Reviews" folder; *Southern Israelite,* 17 November 1939; sermons, 22 September 1941, 12 September 1942, 30 September 1943, 20 September 1950, "High Holidays Sermons" folder; 7 November 1969, 21 November 1969, "Friday Night" folder; 14 December 1938, "Democracy (Barbarism in Germany)"; 26 October 1967, "Succoth (Shemini Atzereth)."

24. Term paper, "The Kabbalah," Emory University, Fall 1929, "Academic Studies—Mysticism" folder; see also 7 May 1974, "O.R.T." folder; Epstein/Bauman interview; 16 June 1962, "Activities—Montreal, Ca" folder.

25. *Atlanta Constitution,* 11 March 1935; undated sermons, 1963–64(?); 17 December 1931, Emory University, Philosophy 311, Fall 1931 (p. 4), "Academic Coursework—Philosophy of Values" folder.

26. See Chaim Grade, *The Yeshiva,* trans. by Curt Leviant, 2 vols. (Indianapolis, Ind.: Bobbs, Merrill, 1976/1977). This analogy was kindly brought to my attention by Professor Pamela Nadell. See also Noveck, *Steinberg.*

27. *Eternal Light,* 125, 123; 2 December 1935, sisterhood culturals, "Development of Jewish Life" folder; undated sermon fragments, "Friday Night misc. notes" folder; sermons, 1961, 1962(?), "Saturday Morning Sermons, undated" folder.

28. On this and following, see Kuhn manuscript; undated article, c. 1976(?) *Southern Israelite*, in "Epstein, Reva 1976" folder; Epstein/Bauman interview; *Chicago Chronicle*, 18 January 1929; *Atlanta Journal*, 14 February 1940; *Southern Israelite*, 3 September 1982; "Chachesman" folder; "Chicago, Illinois" folder.

29. Miscellaneous sermons (1941–45), "Friday Night" folder; 11 November 1959, Emory University Hillel Religious Emphasis Week, "Emory University" folder.

30. On this and following, see 4 April 1964, "Passover Sermons" folder; "Derelicts in Life," undated sermon, 1935 (?), "Friday Night" folder.

31. Joselit, *New York's Jewish Jews;* Noveck, *Steinberg;* Weinstein, *Goldman* George Kranzler, *Williamsburg: A Jewish Community in Transition* (New York: Philipp Feldheim, 1961); Egon Mayer, *Suburb to Shtetl: The Jews of Boro Park* (Philadelphia: Temple University Press, 1979); Israel Rubin, *Satmar: An Island in the City* (Chicago: Quadrangle Press, 1972); Max Halpert, *The Jews of Brownsville, 1880–1925* (D.H.L., Yeshiva University, 1958).

Chapter 7. On Highs and Lows

1. Speech, 1 November 1966, "Sisterhood Adult Education" folder; 12 November 1958, Emory University's Presbyterian Student Forum; 6 May 1953, Emory Christian Association Dinner, "Emory University" folder. Epstein cited "Knowledge—Morality—Peace" as virtually synonymous ideals. Compare and contrast Epstein's thought with that of a conservative Protestant in Mark K. Bauman, *Warren A. Candler: Conservative Admidst Change* (Metuchen, N.J.: Scarecrow Press, 1981).

2. *Southern Israelite*, 23 May 1952.

3. On this and following, see Epstein/Bauman interview; undated sermon, 1968(?), "Saturday Morning Sermons" folder; *Greenville* (S.C.) *News*, April 1964, Epstein scrapbooks; *Atlanta Constitution*, 20 November 1964; sermons, 11 April 1958, 13 April 1968, 14 April 1964, "Passover Sermons" folder; 27 October 1963, "Adult Classes—Sunday Morning" folder; 16 November 1962, 13 November 1967, 5 April 1968, 3 May 1968, 31 January 1969, 21 February 1969, 14 March 1969, 17 October 1969, 7 November 1969, 27 March 1970, 30 June 1972, 30 November 1973, 18 October 1974, 10 October 1975, 23 April 1976, 11 November 1977, 17 February 1978, 5 March 1976, 9 April 1976, 18 January 1980, "Friday Night" folder; 14 October 1967, 23 September 1968, 2 October 1968, "High Holidays Sermons" folder. The malaise noted for Epstein during the 1950s through the 1970s was not unusual among his rabbinic peers. See, for example, Jerome E. Carlin and Saul H. Mendlovitz, "The American Rabbi: A Religious Specialist Responds to Loss of Authority," in Marshall Sklare, ed., *The Jews: Social Patterns of an American Group* (Glencoe, Ill.: Free Press, 1958), 377–413; Salo W. Baron, "The Image of the Rabbi, Formerly and Today," in Jeanette Meisel Baron, ed., *Steeled in Adversity: Essays and Addresses on American Jewish Life* (Philadelphia: Jewish Publication Society, 1971); Bloom, "Rabbi as Symbolic Exemplar"; Jacob K. Shankman, "The Changing Role of The Rabbi," in Bertram W. Korn, ed., *Retrospect and Prospect* (New York: Central Conference of American Rabbis, 1965); Eli Ginzberg, "The Rabbi's Multi-Faceted Role—A Study in Conflict and Resolution," in *On Being a Rabbi* (New York: Herbert H. Lehman Institute of Ethics Conference, 1964); Raphael posits a shift in power in Zionist ranks around 1948 from Abba Hillel Silver and the pulpit to the welfare funds, federations, and community control in *Silver*, 175–82.

4. Arnold Shankman, "Atlanta Jewry, 1900–1930," *American Jewish Archives*

(1973), 154, table 1; Jay Weinstein, *et al.*, "Metropolitan Atlanta Jewish Population Study: Summary of Major Findings" (pamphlet; Atlanta: Atlanta Jewish Federation, 1985); telephone interview with Mike Gettinger by this author, 13 November 1986; Epstein/Bauman interview. On the modern federation, philanthropy, and changes in power and roles, see Elazar, *Community and Polity;* Bauman, "Emergence of Jewish Social Services"; Raphael, *History of the United Jewish Appeal.*

5. Epstein/Bauman interview; Epstein/Herbert Karp correspondence, 25 December 1978, 21 March 1979, 2 November 1981, 14 December 1981, 11 January 1982, 25 February 1982, "Retirement" folder; Israel Stark to Harry H. Epstein, n.d., 1964(?), "Chicago, Illinois" folder.

Overview and Conclusion

1. On this and following, see "Rabbi, Rabbinate," *Encyclopaedia Judaica,* vol. 13, 1446–58; Malcolm Stern, "Role of the Rabbi"; Raphael, *Profiles,* 128–30.

2. On this and following, see Thomas Kessner, "Gershom Mendes Seixas: His Religious 'Calling,' Outlook and Competence," *American Jewish History* (June 1969), 445–71. Jacob Rader Marcus, *The Handsome Young Man in the Black Gown: The Personal World of Gershom Seixas* (Cincinnati, Ohio: Hebrew Union College Press, 1970); David and Tamar de Sola Pool, *An Old Faith in the New World; Portrait of Shearith Israel, 1654–1954* (New York: Columbia University Press, 1955); Morris A. Gutstein, *The Story of the Jews of Newport: Two and a Half Centuries of Judaism, 1658–1908* (New York: Bloch, 1936); Barnett A. Elzas, *The Jews of South Carolina from the Earliest Times to the Present Day* (Philadelphia: Jewish Publication Society, 1905); Charles Reznikoff, *The Jews of Charleston* (Philadelphia: Jewish Publication Society, 1950); Saul J. Rubin, *Third to None: The Saga of Savannah Jewry, 1733–1983* (Savannah: privately published, 1983); Edwin Wolf and Maxwell Whiteman, *The History of The Jews of Philadelphia from Colonial Times to the Age of Jackson* (Philadelphia: Jewish Publication Society, 1975); Myron Berman, *Richmond's Jewry, 1769–1976, Shabbat in Shockoe* (Charlottesville: University Press of Virginia for the Jewish Community Federation of Richmond, 1979); Bernard D. Weinryb, "Jewish Immigration and Accommodation to America," *Publications of the American Jewish Historical Society* (May–June 1957).

3. Leon Jick, *The Americanization of the Synagogue, 1820–1870* (Hanover, N.H.: University Press of New England for Brandeis University Press, 1976); Lance J. Sussman, "Isaac Leeser and the Protestantization of American Judaism," *American Jewish Archives* (April 1986), 1–22; Israel Tabak, "Rabbi Abraham Rice of Baltimore: Pioneer of Orthodox Judaism in America," *Tradition* (Summer 1965), 100–120; Stern, "Role of the Rabbi"; Isaac M. Fein, *The Making of an American Jewish Community: The History of Baltimore Jewry from 1773 to 1920* (Philadelphia: Jewish Publication Society, 1971).

4. Goldman, *Giants of Faith;* Stephen Gross Mostov, "A 'Jerusalem' on the Ohio: The Social and Economic History of Cincinnati's Jewish Community, 1840–1875," (Ph.D. diss., Brandeis University, 1981). For the conflicting experiences of Gustavus Poznanski, see Solomon Breibert, *The Rev. Mr. Gustavus Poznanski: First American Jewish Reform Minister* (Charleston: privately printed, 1979); Robert Liberles, "Conflict Over Reform: The Case of Congregation Beth Elohim, Charleston, South Carolina," in Wertheimer, ed., *American Synagogue,* 274–96.

5. On this and following, see George L. Mosse, *German Jews Beyond Judaism* (Cincinnati, Ohio: Hebrew Union College Press, 1985); Todd M. Endelman, *The Jews of Georgian England, 1714–1830* (Philadelphia: Jewish Publication Society, 1979);

Arthur Barnett, *The Western Synagogue through Two Centuries (1761–1961)* (London: Valentine-Mitchell, 1961); Charles Duschinsky, *The Rabbinate of the Great Synagogue, London, From 1756 to 1842* (London: 1921; Westmead, Farnborough and Hants, 1971); Arthur Hertzberg, *The French Enlighenment and the Jews* (New York: KTAV, 1968) (especially pp. 334–53); Ismar Schorsch, "Zacharias Frankel," 344–54; Max Gruenewald, "The Modern Rabbi," *The Leo Baeck Institute Yearbook,* vol. 2 (London: East and West Library, 1957), 85–91; Alexander Altman, "The New Style of Preaching in Nineteenth-Century German Jewry," Alexander Altman, ed., *Studies in Nineteenth-Century Jewish Intellectual History* (Cambridge: Harvard University Press, 1964), 65–116; Michael A. Meyer, "Christian Influence on Early German Reform Judaism," Charles Berlin, ed., *Studies in Jewish Bibliography, History and Literature* (New York: KTAV, 1971), 289–301; Norman Cohen, "Non Religious Factors in the Emergence of the Chief Rabbinate," *Transactions of the Jewish Historical Society of England* 21 (1962–1967), 304–13; Lance J. Sussman, "Taanim [*sic*], Hazzanim, and Doctor-Rabbi," *Keeping Posted* (April 1988), 3–7.

6. Goldman, *Giants of Faith;* Israel Knox, *Rabbi in America: The Story of Isaac M. Wise* (Boston and Toronto: Little, Brown, 1957); Jacob R. Marcus, *The Americanization of I. M. Wise* (Cincinnati, Ohio: Hebrew Union College, 1931); James G. Heller, *Isaac M. Wise: His Life, Work, and Thought* (New York: Union of American Hebrew Congregations, 1965); Sussman, "Lesser"; Bertram W. Korn, "Isaac Lesser: Centennial Reflections," *American Jewish Archives* (November 1967), 127–41; Maxwell Whitehead, "Isaac Leeser and the Jews of Philadelphia," *Publications of the American Jewish Historical Society* (June 1959), 207–44; Urofsky, *Voice that Spoke for Justice;* Carl Hermann Voss, "The Lion and the Lamb—An Evaluation of the Life and Work of Stephen S. Wise," *American Jewish Archives* (April 1969), 3–19; Robert D. Shapiro, "A Reform Rabbi in the Progressive Era: The Early Career of Stephen S. Wise" (Ph.D. diss., Harvard University, 1984).

7. Raphael, *Profiles;* Bernstein, "Emergence"; idem., "Generational Conflict"; Gurock, "Resisters and Accommodators"; Davis, *Emergence of Conservative Judaism;* Emma Felsenthal, *Bernard Felsenthal: Teacher in Israel* (New York: Oxford University Press, 1924); David de Sola Pool, *H. Pereira Mendes* (New York: Columbia University Press,1938); Gurock, "From Exception to Role Mode," 456–84; Bernard Drachman, *The Unfailing Light* (New York: Rabbinical Council of America, 1948); Goldman, *Giants of Faith;* Max Nussenbaum, "Champion of Orthodox Judaism: A Biography of Reverend Sabato Morais," (D.H.L. diss., Bernard Revel Graduate School of Yeshiva University, 1964); Wolf and Whiteman, *Jews of Philadelphia;* Murray Friedman, ed., *Jewish Life in Philadelphia, 1830–1940* (Philadelphia: ISHI, 1983); Samuel M. Cohen, "Kaufmann Kohler (1843–1926)," in Noveck, *Great Jewish Thinkers,* 227–52; William W. Blood, *Apostle of Reason: A Biography of Joseph Krauskopf* (Philadelphia: Dorrance, 1973); David Einhorn Hirsch, *Rabbi Emil G. Hirsch: The Reform Advocate* (Chicago: Whitehall, 1968); Harold S. Wechsler, "Pulpit or Professoriate: The Case of Morris Jastrow," *American Jewish History* (June 1985), 338–55.

8. Sarna, "Introduction"; Shankman, "Changing Roles"; Robert V. Friedenberg, *"Hear O Israel": The History of American Jewish Preaching, 1654–1970* (Tuscaloosa and London: University of Alabama Press, 1989); Altman, *Essays,* 190–245; Gruenewald, "Modern Rabbi," 85–97; Jick, *Americanization of the Synagogue;* Sussman, "Lesser," 8. On rabbinic activism and its limits in the South, see Stern, "Role of the Rabbi" (especially p. 26); Cowitt, *Birmingham's Rabbi;* Blumberg, *One Voice.* On social service agencies, see Bauman, "Emergence of Jewish Social Service Agencies"; *idem.* and Shankman, "Rabbi as Ethnic Broker."

9. See Eli Evans, *The Provincials: A Personal History of Jews in the South* (New

York: Atheneum, 1973); in Atlanta the terms of rabbis who served in the same pulpit before being granted emeritus status during this era were as follows: Marx for fifty-four years, Epstein for fifty-five years, Geffen for forty-seven years, and Cohen for thirty-five years. Rubin, *Satmar*; Nissan Mindel, *Rabbi Joseph I. Schneersohn* (New York: Kehot, 1947).

10. Mark K. Bauman, review, Ziff, ed., *Lev Tuviah, American Jewish Archives* (forthcoming); Rakeffet-Rothkoff, *Silver Era;* Alon, "Lithuanian Yeshivas."

11. Abraham J. Karp, "New York Chooses a Chief Rabbi," *Publications of the American Jewish Historical Society* (March 1955), 129–94; Rothkoff, "American Sojourn of Ridbaz," 557–72; Hyman B. Grinstein, "The Efforts of East European Jewry to Organize Its Own Community in the United States," *Publications of the American Jewish Historical Society* (1959), 73–89; Arthur Goren, *New York Jews and the Quest for Community* (New York: Columbia University Press, 1970); Gurock, *When Harlem Was Jewish*; Rakeffet-Rothkoff, *Silver Era;* Kaganoff, "Orthodox Rabbinate"; Raphael, *Profiles;* Gurock, "Resisters and Accommodators"; Goldman, *Giants of Faith.*

12. Raphael, *Profiles* (especially p. 68); Klaperman, *Yeshiva University;* Davis, *Conservative Judaism;* Sklare, *Conservative Judaism;* Eli Ginzberg, *Keeper of the Law: Louis Ginzberg* (Philadelphia: Jewish Publication Society, 1966); Baila Round Shargel, *Practical Dreamer: Israel Friedlaender and the Shaping of American Judaism* (New York: Jewish Theological Seminary, 1985); Carlin and Mendlovitz, "American Rabbi"; Shankman, "Changing Role"; Baron, "Image of the Rabbi"; Robert Gordis, *An American Jewish Philosophy: Conservative Judaism* (New York: Behrman House, 1945); Goldman, *Giants of Faith;* Aharon Lichtenstein, "R. Joseph Soloveitchek (1903–)," in Noveck, ed., *Great Jewish Thinkers,* 281–97; Rothkoff, *Revel;* Hoenig, *Revel;* Abraham J. Karp. "Solomon Schecter Comes to America," *American Jewish Historical Quarterly* (September 1963), 42–62; Norman Bentwich, *Solomon Schecter* (New York: Bloch, 1948); Libowitz, *Kaplan;* Eisenstein and Kohn, *Kaplan;* Noveck, *Steinberg;* Weinstein, *Goldman;* Deborah Dash Moore, *B'nai B'rith and the Challenges of Ethnic Leadership* (Albany: State University Press of New York, 1981); Philip Bernstein, *To Dwell in Unity: The Jewish Federation Movement in America, 1960–1980* (Philadelphia: Jewish Publication Society, 1984).

13. On this and following, see Joseph Lookstein, "Neo-Hasidism of Abraham Heschel," *Judaism* (Summer 1956); Maurice Friedman, "Abraham J. Heschel: Toward a Philosophy of Judaism," *Conservative Judaism* (Winter 1956); Raphael, *Silver.*

14. Bloom, "Rabbi as Symbolic Exemplar"; Abraham J. Feldman, *The American Reform Rabbi: A Profile of a Profession* (New York: Bloch, 1965); Polner, *Rabbi.*

15. Bloom, "Rabbi as Symbolic Exemplar"; Bauman and Shankman, "Rabbi as Ethnic Broker"; Bauman, "Role Theory and History"; Victor R. Greene, *American Immigrant Leaders, 1800–1910* (Baltimore: Johns Hopkins University Press, 1987); Sarna, "Spectrum"; Arthur Mann, *Yankee Reformers in the Urban Age: Social Reform in Boston, 1880–1900* (New York: Harper and Row, 1954); Benny Kraut, *From Reform Judaism to Ethical Culture: The Religious Evolution of Felix Adler* (Cincinnati, Ohio: Hebrew Union College, 1979); Pamela S. Nadell, "Conservative Rabbis as Ethnic Leaders," *Judaism* (Summer 1990), 345–65.

Bibliography

Manuscript Collections

Atlanta. Jewish Community Archives of the Jewish Heritage Center, Atlanta Jewish Federation. Harry H. Epstein Collection.

Atlanta. Special Collections. Woodruff Library, Emory University. Jacob M. Rothschild Collection.

Interviews

Epstein, Harry H. Conducted by Mark K. Bauman. June–July 1986. 15 November 1989.

Epstein, Harry H. Conducted by Cliff Kuhn. ca. 1985.

Geffen, David. Conducted by Mark K. Bauman. 10 October 1986.

Gettinger, Max "Mike." Conducted by Mark K. Bauman. 16 June 1986.

Goldstein, Doris. Conducted by Mark K. Bauman. 12 August 1986.

Mesch, Barry. Conducted by Mark K. Bauman. 15 November 1986.

Mesch, Vellie. Conducted by Mark K. Bauman. 17 November 1986. 24 November 1986.

Sanders, Herte. Conducted by Cliff Kuhn. ca. 1985.

Secondary Sources

Abelson, Saul. "Chicago's Hebrew Theological College." Union of Orthodox Congregations of America *Yearbook*. 1947: 160–68.

Abramovitch, Raphael. "The Jewish Socialist Movement in Russia and Poland (1897–1919)." In *The Russian People: Past and Present*. Vol. 2. New York: Central Yiddish Culture Organization, 1948.

Altman, Alexander. "The New Style of Preaching in Nineteenth-Century German Jewry." In *Studies in Nineteenth-Century Jewish Intellectual History*. Edited by Alexander Altman. Cambridge: Harvard University Press, 1964.

Angus, Jacob B. "Abraham Isaac Kuk (1865–1935)." In *Great Jewish Thinkers of the Twentieth Century*. Edited by Simon Novak. N.p.: B'nai B'rith Department of Adult Education, 1963.

———. *High Priest of Rebirth: The Life, Times, and Thought of Abraham Isaac Kuk.* 2d ed. New York: Bloch, 1946.

———. "The Orthodox Stream." *Guideposts in Modern Judaism.* New York: Bloch, 1954. Reprinted in *Understanding American Judaism.* Vol. 2. Edited by Jacob Neusner. New York: KTAV, 1975.

Barnett, Arthur. *The Western Synagogue Through Two Centuries (1761–1961)*. London: Valentine-Mitchell, 1961.

Baron, Salo W. "The Image of the Rabbi, Formerly and Today." In *Steeled In Adversity: Essays and Addresses on American Jewish Life.* Edited by Jeanette Meisel Baron. Philadelphia: Jewish Publication Society, 1971.

Brauer, Yehuda. *American Jewry and the Holocaust*. Detroit: Wayne State University Press, 1981.

————. *My Brother's Keepers: A History of the American Jewish Joint Distribution Committee, 1929–1939*. Philadelphia: Jewish Publication Society, 1974.

Bauman, Mark K. "Centripetal and Centrifugal Forces Facing the People of Many Communities: Atlanta Jewry from the Leo Frank Case to the Great Depression." *Atlanta Historical Journal*, Fall 1979, 25–54.

————. "The Emergence of Jewish Social Service Agencies in Atlanta." *Georgia Historical Quarterly*, Winter 1985, 488–508.

————. "Harry H. Epstein and the Adaptation of Second Generation East European Jews in Atlanta." *American Jewish Archives*, Fall/Winter 1990, 133–46.

————. "Role Theory and History: Ethnic Brokerage in the Atlanta Jewish Community." *American Jewish History*, September 1983, 71–95.

————. "Victor H. Kriegshaber, Community Builder." *American Jewish History*, Autumn 1989, 94–110.

————. *Warren A. Candler: Conservative Amidst Change*. Metuchen, N. J.: Scarecrow Press, 1981.

————. Review of *Lev Tuviah* by Joel Ziff. *American Jewish Archives*. Forthcoming.

Bentwich, Norman. *Solomon Schecter*. New York: Bloch, 1948.

Berkow, Ira. *Maxwell Street: Survival in a Bazaar*. Garden City, N.Y.: Doubleday, 1977.

Berman, Myron. *Richmond's Jewry, 1769–1976, Shabbat in Shockoe*. Charlottesville: University Press of Virginia for the Jewish Community Federation of Richmond, 1979.

Bernstein, Louis. "The Emergence of the English Speaking Orthodox Rabbinate." Ph.D. diss., Bernard Revel Graduate School of Yeshiva University, 1977.

————. "Generational Conflict in American Orthodoxy: The Early Years of the Rabbinical Council of America." *American Jewish History*, December 1979, 226–33.

Bernstein, Philip. *To Dwell in Unity: The Jewish Federation Movement in America, 1960–1980*. Philadelphia: Jewish Publication Society, 1984.

Beton, Sol, ed. *Sephardim and a History of Congregation Or VeShalom*. Atlanta: Congregation Or VeShalom, 1981.

Blood, William W. *Apostle of Reason: A Biography of Joseph Krauskopf*. Philadelphia: Dorrance, 1973.

Bloom, Jacob. "The Rabbi as Symbolic Exemplar." Ph.D. diss., Columbia University, 1972.

Blumberg, Janice R. *One Voice: Rabbi Jacob M. Rothschild and the Troubled South*. Macon, Ga.: Mercer University Press, 1985.

Borsten, Orin. "Modernizing Traditional Judaism." *Southern Israelite* (September 1936).

Breibart, Solomon. *The Rev. Mr. Gustavus Poznanski: First American Jewish Reform Minister*. Charleston, S.C.: n.p., 1979.

Carlin, Jerome E. and Mendlovitz, Saul H. "The American Rabbi: A Religious Specialist Responds to Loss of Authority." In *The Jews: Social Patterns of an American Group*. Edited by Marshall Sklare. Glencoe, Ill.: Free Press, 1958.

Cohen, Naomi W. *The Year after the Riots: American Response to the Palestine Crisis of 1929–1930*. Detroit: Wayne State University Press, 1987.

Cohen, Norman. "Non-Religious Factors in the Emergence of the Chief Rabbinate." *Transactions of the Jewish Historical Society of England*, 1962–67, 304–13.

Cohon, Samuel M. "Kaufman Kohler (1843–1926)." In *Great Jewish Thinkers of the Twentieth Century*. Edited by Simon Noveck. N.p.: B'nai B'rith Department of Adult Education, 1963.

Cowett, Mark. *Birmingham's Rabbi: Morris Newfield and Alabama, 1895–1940*. University: University of Alabama Press, 1986.

Davis, Moshe. *The Emergence of Conservative Judaism: The Historical School in Nineteenth Century America*. Philadelphia: Jewish Publication Society, 1963.

Drachman, Bernard. *The Unfailing Light*. New York: Rabbinical Council of America, 1948.

Duschinsky, Charles. *The Rabbinate of the Great Synagogue, London, from 1756 to 1842*. London: Westmead, Farnborough and Hants, 1971.

Eisen, Arnold M. *The Chosen People: A Study in Jewish Religious Ideology*. Bloomington: Indiana University Press, 1983.

———. *Galut: Modern Jewish Reflections on Homelessness and Homecoming*. Bloomington: Indiana University Press, 1986.

Eisenstein, Ira. "Mordecai M. Kaplan (1881–)." In *Great Jewish Thinkers of the Twentieth Century*. Edited by Simon Noveck. N.p.: B'nai B'rith Department of Adult Education, 1963.

———, and Kohn, Eugene. *Mordecai M. Kaplan: An Evaluation*. New York: Reconstructionist Press, 1952.

Elazar, Daniel. *Community and Polity: The Organizational Dynamics of American Jewry*. Philadelphia: Jewish Publication Society, 1976.

Ellenson, David. "Rabbi Esriel Hildesheimer and the Quest for Religious Authority." *Modern Judaism*, December 1981, 279–97.

———. "A Response by Modern Orthodoxy to Jewish Religious Pluralism: The Case of Esriel Hildesheimer." *Tradition*, Spring 1979, 74–90.

Elzas, Barnett A. *The Jews of South Carolina from the Earliest Times to the Present Day*. Philadelphia: Jewish Publication Society, 1905.

Elovitz, Mark H. *A Century of Jewish Life in Dixie: The Birmingham Experience*. University: University of Alabama Press, 1974.

Endelman, Todd M. *The Jews of Georgian England, 1714–1830*. Philadelphia: Jewish Publication Society, 1979.

Epstein, Harry H. "The Basis of Religious Certainty in Judaism: A Study of Six Sources." M.A. thesis, Emory University, 1932.

———. *Judaism and Progress: Sermons and Addresses*. New York: Bloch, 1935.

"Epstein, Harry Hyman." *Who's Who in World Jewry*. Tel Aviv: Olive Books, 1955.

"Epstein, Moses Mordecai." *Encyclopaedia Judaica*. Vol. 6, 835–36.

Evans, Eli. *The Provincials: A Personal History of Jews in the South*. New York: Atheneum, 1973.

Fasman, Oscar Z. "After Fifty Years, An Optimist." *American Jewish History*, December 1979, 159–73.

Fein, Isaac M. *The Making of an American Jewish Community: The History of Baltimore Jewry from 1773 to 1920*. Philadelphia: Jewish Publication Society, 1971.

Feingold, Henry L. "Courage First and Intelligence Second: The American Jewish Secular Elite, Roosevelt and the Failure to Rescue." *American Jewish History*, June 1983, 424–60.

Feldman, Abraham J. *The American Reform Rabbi: A Profile of a Profession*. New York: Bloch, 1965.

Felsenthal, Emma. *Bernard Felsenthal: Teacher in Israel*. New York: Oxford University Press, 1924.

Frankel, Jonathan. *Prophecy and Politics: Socialism, Nationalism and the Russian Jew, 1862–1917*. New York: Cambridge University Press, 1981.

Friedenberg, Robert V. *"Hear O Israel": The History of American Jewish Preaching, 1654–1970*. Tuscaloosa and London: University of Alabama Press, 1989.

Friederman, Joseph. "A Concise History of Agudah Israel." In *Yaacov Rosenheim Memorial Volume*. New York, 1963.

Friedman, Maurice. "Abraham J. Heschel: Toward a Philosophy of Judaism." *Conservative Judaism*, Winter 1956.

Friedman, Murray, ed. *Jewish Life in Philadelphia, 1830–1940*. Philadelphia: ISHI, 1983.

Gal, Allon. "The Mission Motif in American Zionism (1898–1948)." *American Jewish History*, June 1986, 41–64.

Ganin, Zvi. *Truman, American Jewry and Israel, 1945–1948*. New York: Holmes and Meier, 1979.

Geffen, David. "The Literary Legacy of Rabbi Tobias Geffen in Atlanta, 1910–1970." *Atlanta Historical Journal*, Fall 1979, 85–90.

Geffen, Sara J. "The Academies of Kovno and Slobodka." In *Lev Tuviah*. Edited by Joel Ziff. Privately published, 1988.

Geldbart, Lisa. "A Conversation with Rabbi Epstein." *Southern Israelite*, 24 March 1978.

Ginzberg, Eli. *Keeper of the Law: Louis Ginzberg*. Philadelphia: Jewish Publication Society, 1966.

———. "The Rabbi's Multi-Faceted Role—A Study in Conflict and Resolution." In *On Being a Rabbi*. New York: Herbert H. Lehman Institute of Ethics Conference, 1964.

Ginzberg, Louis. *Students, Scholars and Saints*. Philadelphia: Jewish Publication Society, 1928.

Gold, Carolyn. "When Bat Mitzvahs Began." *Southern Israelite*, 18 July 1986.

Goldberg, Hillel. *Between Berlin and Slobodka*. Hoboken, N.J.: KTAV, 1989.

———. "Israel Salanter's Suspended Conversation." *Tradition*, Fall 1986, 31–43.

———. *Israel Salanter: Text, Structure, Idea*. New York: KTAV, 1982.

Goldman, Alex J. *Giants of Faith: Great American Rabbis*. New York: Citadel Press, 1964.

Goldstein, Doris H. *From Generation to Generation: A Centennial History of Ahavath Achim, 1887–1987*. Atlanta: Capricorn Press, 1987.

Gordis, Robert. *An American Jewish Philosophy: Conservative Judaism*. New York: Behrman House, 1945.

Goren, Arthur. *New York Jews and the Quest for Community.* New York: Columbia University Press, 1970.

Grade, Chaim. *The Yeshiva.* 2 vols. Translated by Curt Leviant. Indianapolis, Ind.: Bobbs, Merrill, 1976/1977.

Greene, Victor. *American Immigrant Leaders, 1800–1910.* Baltimore: Johns Hopkins University Press, 1986.

Grinstead, Hyman B. "The Efforts of East European Jewry to Organize Its Own Community in the United States." *Publications of the American Jewish Historical Society,* 1959, 73–89.

Grose, Peter. *Israel in the Mind of America.* New York: Knopf, 1983.

Gruenewald, Max. "The Modern Rabbi." In *The Leo Baeck Institute Yearbook.* Vol. 2. London: East and West Library, 1957.

Gurock, Jeffrey S. "From Exception to Role Model: Bernard Drachman and the Evolution of Jewish Religious Life in America, 1880–1920." *American Jewish History,* June 1987, 456–84.

———. *The Men and Women of Yeshiva: Higher Education, Orthodoxy, and American Judaism.* New York: Columbia University Press, 1989.

———. "Resisters and Accommodators: Varieties of Orthodox Rabbis in America, 1886–1983." *American Jewish Archives,* November 1983, 100–187.

———. "A Stage in the Emergence of the Americanized Synagogue among East European Jews: 1890–1910." *Journal of American Ethnic History,* Spring 1990, 7–25.

———. *When Harlem Was Jewish, 1870–1930.* New York: Columbia University Press, 1975.

Gutstein, Morris A. *The Story of the Jews of Newport: Two and a Half Centuries of Judaism, 1658–1908.* New York: Bloch, 1936.

Halpern, Ben. *The Idea of a Jewish State.* 2d ed. Cambridge: Harvard University Press, 1961.

Halpern, Samuel. *The Political World of American Zionism.* Detroit: Wayne State University Press, 1961.

Halpert, Max. *The Jews of Brownsville, 1880–1925.* D.H.L. thesis, Yeshiva University, 1958.

Handlin, Oscar. *A Continuing Task: The American Jewish Joint Distribution Committee, 1914–1964.* New York: Random House, 1964.

Heller, James G. *Isaac M. Wise: His Life, Work, and Thought.* New York: Union of American Hebrew Congregations, 1965.

Helmreich, William B. *The World of the Yeshiva: An Intimate Portrait of Orthodox Judaism.* New York: Free Press, 1982.

Hertzberg, Arthur. *The French Enlightenment and the Jews.* New York: KTAV, 1968.

———. *The Zionist Idea.* New York: Herzl Press and Doubleday, 1959.

Hertzberg, Steven. *Strangers within the Gate City: Jews of Atlanta, 1845–1915.* Philadelphia: Jewish Publication Society, 1978.

Higham, John. ed. *Ethnic Leadership in America.* Baltimore: Johns Hopkins University Press, 1978.

Hirsch, David Einhorn. *Rabbi Emil G. Hirsch: The Reform Advocate.* Chicago: Whitehall, 1968.

Hoenig, Sidney B. *The Scholarship of Dr. Bernard Revel.* New York: Yeshiva University Press, 1968.

Hofstadter, Richard. *Social Darwinism in American Thought*. Philadelphia: University of Pennsylvania Press, 1944.

Hopkins, Charles Howard. *The Rise of the Social Gospel in American Protestantism*. New Haven: Yale University Press, 1940.

Hyman, Joseph C. *Twenty-five Years of American Aid to Jews Overseas*. Philadelphia: Jewish Publication Society, 1939.

Jick, Leon. *The Americanization of the Synagogue, 1820–1870*. Hanover, N.H.: University Press of New England for Brandeis University Press, 1976.

Joselit, Jenna Weissman. *New York's Jewish Jews: The Orthodox Community in the Interwar Years*. Bloomington and Indianapolis: Indiana University Press, 1990.

Jung, Leo. *The Path of a Pioneer: The Autobiography of Leo Jung*. New York: Soncino, 1980.

Kaganoff, Nathan. "An Orthodox Rabbinate in the South: Tobias Geffen, 1870–1970." *American Jewish History*, September 1983, 56–70.

Kahan, Arcadius. *Essays in Jewish Social and Economic History*. Edited by Roger Weiss. Chicago and London: University of Chicago Press, 1986.

Karp, Abraham J. "The Conservative Rabbi—Dissatisfied But Not Unhappy." *American Jewish Archives*, November 1983, 188–262.

———. "New York Chooses a Chief Rabbi." *Publications of the American Jewish Historical Society*, March 1955, 129–94.

———. "Solomon Schecter Comes to America." *American Jewish Historical Quarterly*, September 1963, 42–62.

Kauffman, Christopher J. *Tradition and Transformation in Catholic Culture*. New York: Macmillan, 1987.

"Kaunas." *Encyclopaedia Judaica*. Vol. 10, 846–50.

Kessner, Thomas. "Gershom Mendes Seixas: His Religious 'Calling,' Outlook and Competence." *American Jewish History*, June 1969, 445–71.

Klaperman, Gilbert. *The Story of Yeshiva University: The First Jewish University in America*. London: Macmillan, 1969.

Knox, Israel. *Rabbi in America: The Story of Isaac M. Wise*. Boston and Toronto: Little, Brown, 1957.

"Kook (Kuk), Abraham Isaac." *Encyclopaedia Judaica*. Vol. 10, 1182–87.

Korn, Bertram W. "Isaac Leeser: Centennial Reflections." *American Jewish Archives*, November 1967, 127–41.

Kranzler, George. *Williamsburg: A Jewish Community in Transition*. New York: Philipp Feldheim, 1961.

Krause, Allen. "Rabbis and Negro Rights in the South, 1954–1967." *American Jewish Archives*, 1969, 20–47.

Kraut, Benny. *From Reform Judaism to Ethical Culture: The Religious Evolution of Felix Adler*. Cincinnati, Ohio: Hebrew Union College, 1979.

Liberles, Robert. "Conflict Over Reform: The Case of Congregation Beth Elohim, Charleston, South Carolina." *The American Synagogue: A Sanctuary Transformed*. Edited by Jack Wertheimer. New York: Cambridge University Press, 1987.

Libowitz, Richard. "Mordecai M. Kaplan as Redactor." Ph.D. diss., Temple University, 1978.

Lichtenstein, Aharon. "R. Joseph Soloveitchek (1903–   )." In *Great Jewish Thinkers of the Twentieth Century*. Edited by Simon Noveck. N.p.: B'nai B'rith Department of Adult Education, 1963.

Liebman, Charles S. "The Training of American Rabbis." In *American Jewish Yearbook*. 1968. Edited by Morris Fine and Milton Himmelfarb. New York: American Jewish Committee, 1968.

"Lithuania." *Encyclopaedia Judaica*. Vol. 11, 365–80.

Lookstein, Joseph. "Neo-Hasidism of Joshua Heschel." *Judaism*, Summer 1956, 248–55.

Mahler, Raphael. *Hasidism and the Jewish Enlightenment: Their Confrontation in Galicia and Poland in the First Half of the Nineteenth Century*. Philadelphia: Jewish Publication Society, 1985.

Mann, Arthur. *Yankee Reformers in the Urban Age: Social Reform in Boston, 1880–1900*. New York: Harper and Row, 1954.

Marcus, Jacob Rader. *The Americanization of I. M. Wise*. Cincinnati, Ohio: Hebrew Union College, 1931.

———. *The Handsome Young Man in the Black Gown: The Personal World of Gershom Seixas*. Cincinnati, Ohio: Hebrew Union College, 1970.

Markovitz, Eugene. "Henry Pereira Mendes: Architect of the Union of Orthodox Jewish Congregations of America." *American Jewish Historical Quarterly*, March 1966, 364–84.

Mayer, Egon. *Suburb to Shtetl: The Jews of Boro Park*. Philadelphia: Temple University Press, 1979.

McLoughlin, William G. *Modern Revivalism*. New York: Ronald, 1959.

Mead, Sidney. *Lively Experiment*. New York: Harper and Row, 1963.

Medloff, Raphael. *The Deafening Silence: American Jewish Leaders and the Holocaust*. New York: Shapolsky, 1987.

Meites, Hyman L., ed. *History of the Jews of Chicago*. Chicago: Jewish Historical Society of Illinois, 1924.

Mendelsohn, Ezra. *Class Struggle in the Pale*. Cambridge: Cambridge University Press, 1970.

Meyer, Michael A. "Christian Influence on Early Reform Judaism." In *Studies in Jewish Bibliography, History and Literature*. Edited by Charles Berlin. New York: KTAV, 1971.

Mindel, Nissan. *Rabbi Joseph I. Schneersohn*. New York: Kehot, 1947.

Mishkin, Leonard C. "History of the Hebrew Theological College/Bet Hamidrash LaTorah." Hebrew Theological College Sixtieth Anniversary *Journal*, 1982.

———. "The Rabbi Ephraim Epstein Story." Eightieth Birthday Celebration Program, 4 October 1956.

Moore, Deborah Dash. *At Home in America: Second Generation New York Jews*. New York: Columbia University Press, 1981.

———. *B'nai B'rith and the Challenges of Ethnic Leadership*. Albany: State University Press of New York, 1981.

Mosse, George L. *German Jews beyond Judaism*. Cincinnati, Ohio: Hebrew Union College, 1985.

Nadell, Pamela S. "Conservative Rabbis as Ethnic Leaders." *Judaism*, Summer 1990, 345–65.

Niebuhr, Reinhold. *The Children of Light and the Children of Darkness*. New York: Charles Scribner's Sons, 1944.

Noveck, Simon. *Milton Steinberg: Portrait of a Rabbi*. New York: KTAV, 1978.

Nussenbaum, Max. "Champion of Orthodox Judaism: A Biography of Reverend Sabato Morais." D.H.L. diss., Bernard Revel Graduate School of Yeshiva University, 1964.

"Orthodoxy." *Encyclopaedia Judaica.* Vol. 12, 1488.

"Pale of Settlement." *Encyclopaedia Judaica.* Vol. 13, 24–28.

Patai, Raphael. *Tents of Jacob: The Diaspora—Yesterday and Today.* Englewood Cliffs, N.J.: Prentice-Hall, 1971.

Pinsky, Edward. "American Jewish Unity During the Holocaust—The Joint Emergency Committee, 1943." *American Jewish History,* June 1983, 477–94.

Polner, Murray. *Rabbi: The American Experience.* New York: Holt, Rinehart and Winston, 1977.

Pool, David de Sola. *H. Pereira Mendes.* New York: Columbia University Press, 1938.

————, and Pool, Tamar. *An Old Faith in the New World: Portrait of Shearith Israel, 1654–1954.* New York: Columbia University Press, 1955.

Rader, Jack. *By the Skill of Their Hands: The Story Of O.R.T.* Geneva: World O.R.T. Union, 1970.

Rakeffet-Rothkoff, Aaron. "The Kaminetzer Rosh Yeshivah: Rabbi Boruch Ber Leibowitz." *Jewish Life,* July-August 1969, 41–46.

————. "The Last Rabbi of Kovno." *Jewish Life,* March-April 1968, 35–40.

————. "The 'Meitsheter Illui.'" *Jewish Life,* November-December 1967, 29–35.

————. "The Mirrer Rosh Yeshiva." *Jewish Life,* May-June 1969, 41–47.

————. "Reb Yitzchak Blaser: A Mussar Giant." *Jewish Life,* Spring 1976, 43–48.

————. *The Silver Era In American Jewish Orthodoxy: Rabbi Eliezar Silver and His Generation.* New York: Yeshiva University Press, 1981.

————. "The Telsher Rav and Rosh Hayeshiva." *Jewish Life,* September-October 1968, 47–52.

Raphael, Marc Lee. *A History of the United Jewish Appeal, 1939–1982.* Chico, Calif.: Scholars Press, 1982.

————. *Profiles in American Judaism: The Reform, Conservative, Orthodox and Reconstructionist Traditions in Historical Perspective.* San Francisco: Harper and Row, 1984.

————. *Abba Hillel Silver: A Profile in American Judaism.* New York and London: Holmes and Meier, 1989.

Rothkoff, Aaron. "The American Sojourn of Ridbaz: Religious Problems Within the Immigrant Community." *American Jewish Historical Quarterly,* June 1968, 557–72.

————. *Bernard Revel: Builder of American Jewish Orthodoxy.* Philadelphia: Jewish Publication Society, 1972.

Reichel, Aaron I. *The Maverick Rabbi: Rabbi Herbert S. Goldstein and the Institutional Synagogue—"A New Institutional Form."* Norfolk, Va.: Donning, 1984.

Reznikoff, Charles. *The Jews of Charleston.* Philadelphia: Jewish Publication Society, 1950.

Rockaway, Robert A. *The Jews of Detroit, From the Beginning, 1762–1914.* Detroit: Wayne State University Press, 1986.

Roskies, Diane, and Roskies, David. *The Shtetl Book.* New York: KTAV, 1979.

Rothschild, Janice O. *As But a Day: The First Hundred Years, 1867–1967.* Atlanta: Hebrew Benevolent Congregation, 1967.

Rubin, Israel. *Satmar: An Island in the City.* Chicago: Quadrangle Press, 1972.

Rubin, Saul J. *Third to None: The Saga of Savannah Jewry, 1733–1983.* Savannah, Ga.: privately published, 1983.

Sachs, A. S. *Worlds That Passed.* Philadelphia: Jewish Publication Society, 1928.

Sarna, Jonathan D., ed. "The American Rabbinate: A Centennial View." *American Jewish Archives,* November 1983.

———. "The Debate Over Mixed Seating in the American Synagogue." In *The American Synagogue: A Sanctuary Transformed.* Edited by Jack Wertheimer. New York: Cambridge University Press, 1987.

———. "The Spectrum of Jewish Leadership in Ante-Bellum America." *Journal of American Ethnic History,* Spring 1982, 59–67.

Schmidt, Sarah. "Horace M. Kallen and the 'Americanization' of Zionism: In Memoriam." *American Jewish Archives,* April 1976, 59–73.

Schorsch, Ismar. "Zacharias Frankel and the European Origins of Conservative Judaism." *Judaism,* Summer 1981, 344–54.

Schultz, Bella E. "Transmitting the Heritage: Jewish Education in Kansas City." In *Mid-America's Promise: A Profile of Kansas City Jewry.* Edited by Joseph P. Schultz. Kansas City, Mo.: Jewish Community Foundation of Greater Kansas City and American Jewish Historical Society, 1982.

Schultz, Joseph P. "The Consensus of 'Civil Religion': The Religious Life of Kansas City Jewry." In *Mid-America's Promise: A Profile of Kansas City Jewry.* Edited by Joseph P. Schultz. Kansas City, Mo.: Jewish Community Foundation of Greater Kansas City and American Jewish Historical Society, 1982.

Scult, Mel. "The Sociologist as Theologian: The Fundamental Assumptions of Mordecai Kaplan's Thought." *Judaism,* Summer 1976, 345–52.

Senn, Alfred Erich. *The Emergence of Modern Lithuania.* New York: Columbia University Press, 1958.

Shankman, Arnold. "Atlanta Jewry, 1900–1930." *American Jewish Archives,* November 1973, 131–55.

———, and Bauman, Mark. "The Rabbi as Ethnic Broker: The Case of David Marx." *Journal of American Ethnic History,* Spring 1983, 51–68.

Shankman, Jacob K. "The Changing Role of the Rabbi." In *Retrospect and Prospect.* Edited by Bertram W. Korn. New York: Central Conference of American Rabbis, 1965.

Shapiro, Leon. *The History of O.R.T.* Hoboken, N.J.: KTAV, 1980.

Shapiro, Robert D. "A Reform Rabbi in the Progressive Era: The Early Career of Stephen S. Wise." Ph.D. diss., Harvard University, 1984.

Sharfman, I. Harold. *The First Rabbi: Origins of Conflict Between Orthodox and Reform: Jewish Polemic Warfare in Pre–Civil War America.* N.p.: Joseph Simon/Pangloss, 1988.

Shargel, Baila Round. *Practical Dreamer: Israel Friedlaender and the Shaping of American Judaism.* New York: Jewish Theological Seminary, 1985.

Shimoff, Ephraim. *Rabbi Isaac Elchanan Spektor.* New York: Yeshiva University Press, 1959.

Simon, Solomon. *In the Thicket.* Philadelphia: Jewish Publication Society, 1963.

Singer, Isaac Bashevis. *In My Father's Court.* New York: Farrar, Strauss and Giroux, 1966.

Sklare, Marshall. *Conservative Judaism: An American Religious Movement.* New York: Free Press, 1955.

"Slobodka Yeshiva." *Encyclopaedia Judaica.* Vol. 14, 1668–669.

Smith, Harold P. "Hebrew Theological College: Its Impact on Chicago and World Jewry," *Hebrew Theological College Journal,* 1980.

Stein, Kenneth W. *A History of Ahavath Achim Synagogue, 1887–1977.* Atlanta: Standard Press, 1978.

Stern, Malcolm. "The Role of the Rabbi in the South." *Turn to the South.* Edited by Nathan Kaganoff and Melvin Urofsky. Charlottesville: University Press of Virginia for the American Jewish Historical Society, 1979.

Sussman, Lance J. "Isaac Leeser and the Protestantization of American Judaism." *American Jewish Archives,* April 1986, 1–22.

———. "The Life and Career of Isaac Leeser (1806–1868): A Study of American Judaism in Its Formative Period." Ph.D. diss., Hebrew Union College–Jewish Institute of Religion, 1987.

———. "Taanim, Hazzanim, and Doctor-Rabbi." *Keeping Posted,* April 1988, 3–7.

Sutker, Solomon. "The Jews of Atlanta, Their Social Strucure and Leadership Patterns." Ph.D. diss., University of North Carolina, 1950.

Szajkowski, Zosa. "How the Mass Migration to America Began." *Jewish Social Studies,* October 1942, 291–310.

———. "Private and Organized American Jewish Overseas Relief (1914–1918). *American Jewish Historical Quarterly,* September 1967, 52–136.

Tabak, Israel. "Rabbi Abraham Rice of Baltimore: Pioneer of Orthodox Judaism in America." *Tradition,* Summer 1965, 100–120.

Tanenbaum, Marc C. "Zachariah Shuster—A Moral Giant." Typescript eulogy delivered at Riverside Chapel, New York, 17 February 1986.

Tobias, Henry J. *The Jewish Bund in Russia: From Its Origins to 1905.* Stanford, Calif.: Stanford University Press, 1972.

Toll, William. *The Making of an Ethnic Middle Class: Portland Jewry over Four Generations.* Albany: State University of New York Press, 1982.

Urofsky, Melvin I. *American Zionism from Herzl to the Holocaust.* Garden City, N.Y.: Doubleday, 1975.

———. "A Cause in Search of Itself: American Zionism After the State." *American Jewish History,* December 1979, 79–91.

———. *Louis D. Brandeis and the Progressive Tradition.* Boston: Little, Brown, 1981.

———. *A Voice That Spoke for Justice: The Life and Times of Stephen A. Wise.* Albany: State University of New York Press, 1982.

———. *We Are One! American Jewry and Israel.* Garden City, N.Y.: Doubleday, 1978.

Ury, Zalman F. "Salanter's Musar Movement." In *Studies in Judaica.* Edited by Leon D. Stitskin. New York: KTAV, 1972.

Voss, Carl Hermann. "The Lion and the Lamb—An Evaluation of the Life and Work of Stephen S. Wise." *American Jewish Archives,* April 1969, 3–19.

Wechsler, Harold S. "Pulpit or Professoriate: The Case of Morris Jastrow." *American Jewish History,* June 1985, 338–55.

Weinberg, J. J. "The Musar Movement and Lithuanian Jewry." *Men of the Spirit.* Edited by Leo Jung. New York: Kymson, 1964.

Weinryb, Bernard D. "Jewish Immigration and Accommodation to America." *Publications of the American Jewish Historical Society,* May-June 1957, 366–403.

Weinstein, Jacob J. *Solomon Goldman: A Rabbi's Rabbi.* New York: KTAV, 1973.

Weinstein, Jay, *et al.* "Metropolitan Atlanta Jewish Population Study: Summary of Major Findings." Atlanta: Atlanta Jewish Federation, 1985.

Weisser, Michael R. *A Brotherhood of Memory: Jewish Landsmanshaftn in the New World.* New York: Basic Books, 1985.

White, Morton. *Social Thought in America: The Revolt against Formalism.* New York: Viking, 1947.

Whitehead, Maxwell. "Isaac Leeser and the Jews of Philadelphia." *Publications of the American Jewish Historical Society,* June 1959, 207–44.

Wolf, Edwin, and Whitehead, Maxwell. *The History of the Jews of Philadelphia from Colonial Times to the Age of Jackson.* Philadelphia: Jewish Publication Society, 1975.

Woocher, Jonathan S. *Sacred Religion: The Civil Religion of American Jews.* Bloomington: Indiana University Press, 1986.

Wyman, David S. *The Abandonment of the Jews: America and the Holocaust, 1941–1945.* New York: Pantheon, 1984.

Zarchin, Michael M. *Glimpses of Jewish Life in San Francisco.* Oakland, Calif.: Judah L. Magnes Memorial Museum, 1952. Rev. ed., 1964.

Zborowski, Mark, and Herzog, Elizabeth. *Life Is with the People: The Culture of the Shtetl.* New York: Schocken, 1952.

Ziff, Joel, ed. *Lev Tuviah.* N.p.: privately published, 1988.

Zipperstein, Steven. *The Jews of Odessa: A Cultural History, 1794–1881.* Stanford, Calif.: Stanford University Press, 1986.

Index